DARE
TO
CONFRONT!

DARE TO CONFRONT!

How to Intervene When Someone You Care About Has an Alcohol or Drug Problem

◆

BOB WRIGHT
and
DEBORAH GEORGE WRIGHT

MasterMedia Limited
NEW YORK

MASTERMEDIA and colophon are registered trademarks of MasterMedia Limited.

10 9 8 7 6 5 4 3 2 1

Library of Congress Cataloging-in-Publication Data

Wright, Bob, SRN, RMN.
    Dare to confront!: how to intervene when someone you care about
  has an alcohol or drug problem/by Bob Wright and Deborah George
  Wright; with an introduction by Darryl S. Inaba.
      p. cm.
    ISBN: 0-942361-21-0
    1. Alcoholism—United States—Psychological aspects.   2. Narcotic
  addicts—United States—Psychology.   3. Alcoholism—Treatment—
  United States.   4. Drug abuse—Treatment—United States.
  5. Co-dependence (Psychology)—United States.   I. Wright, Deborah
  George. II. Title.
  HV5296.W85   1990
  362.29'13—dc20   90-35710
                                                              CIP

Designed by Stanley S. Drate/Folio Graphics Co. Inc. for Martin Cook Associates

Manufactured in the United States of America

We dedicate
Dare to Confront!
to the memory of Bob Wright, Sr., and all
who lost their lives to a chemical
dependency and without whose experiences
many others would not have a chance to
live. There is a part of each of you
in this book.

"They all surprised me. I really wasn't expecting it. At first I was pretty mad. I thought, 'Who the hell are they to be telling me I have a problem?' As far as I was concerned, *they* were the problem. I'd be fine if they'd get their act together and get out of my face! I really didn't think it was that bad. But they made it pretty clear. They told me a lot of things I did 'wired' that supposedly no one knew about, and a lot of other things that I don't even remember doing! That's when I got scared—really scared. I can't say I wanted recovery. I just wanted out—any way I could find it. I said, 'Okay,' and then started figuring how I could get around it. But they left me without any choices. Either I went with Brad or I lost my wife, my kids, my home, my job and my reputation. It all happened so fast. They told me my bottom was where I chose to make it, but that they had gone as low as they were going to go. They loved me, but it was over. They weren't going to let my screw-ups hurt them any longer. That hit me like a howitzer. No one has ever said anything so straight to me before or since. That was my bottom. What can I say? It worked."

—Recovering cocaine addict/alcoholic

Contents

◆

FOREWORD   xiii
  The Honorable Ruth Lewis Farkas, Ed.D.

PREFACE: Because You Care   xv

ACKNOWLEDGMENTS   xvii

INTRODUCTION: You're Not Alone   xix
  Dr. Darryl S. Inaba, Pharm.D.

PART

I

IT'S A PROBLEM!

1 Had Enough?   3

The abuser doesn't care. You do. It's time to act.

**2 How Can You Tell If There's Really
a Problem?**   13

Is it affecting anyone? Is there evidence?

3 How Far Has It Progressed?   27

There are recognizable patterns.

PART

II

WHAT YOU NEED TO KNOW BEFORE YOU DO ANYTHING

4 What Causes Chemical Dependency?   39
It's a biological disease with psychological effects.

5 What Is an Intervention?   57
Intervention is "tough" love. Three approaches.

6 What Is Recovery?   69
What it means to be weller than well. The promise.

7 What Help Is Available?   77
How to choose the best resource for your situation.

PART

III

CONDUCTING AN INTERVENTION

8 How to Prepare   91
Deciding the "who, what, when and where?"

9 How an Intervention Works   107
Confront, Affirm, Respond and Enact (CARE).

10 Anticipating the Dependent's Response   119
Knowing reaction style can give you the edge.

11 Understanding the Mind Games   135
Some common things are going on.

12 How to Respond to Typical Arguments   143

Be prepared with sound responses.

13 How to Keep the Pressure On   151

Success depends on ultimatums and follow-through.

14 Questions About Recovery That You've Always Wanted to Ask, But . . .   157

15 Enjoying the Rewards   165

Saving a life is the highest human achievement.

APPENDICES

A: DETACHMENT: THE FIRST STEP TO A LOVED ONE'S RECOVERY   171

B: EMOTIONS AND FEELINGS CHECKLIST   175

C: LISTING THE OBJECTIVE FACTS   179

D: ARE YOU CO-DEPENDENT? (CHECKLIST)   181

E: ARE YOU ALCOHOLIC? (CHECKLIST)   187

F: ARE YOU DRUG ADDICTED? (CHECKLIST)   193

BIBLIOGRAPHY   199

INDEX   203

Foreword

◆

With 30 million alcohol and drug addicts, and one out of every three American families affected, it seems we all know, work or live with someone who has a chemical dependency.

Most people want to get involved, but don't know what to do, especially if a professional is not available. This book is a handy, step-by-step reference on how to effectively confront the dependent and convince him or her to get help. It is vital information because addicts cannot intervene on themselves. Moreover, for economic, social or geographic reasons, as many as 85% do not have access to professional interventionists.

At a time when more interventions are needed, even fewer professionals are available to do them. Due to changes and cutbacks in insurance coverage, most treatment centers have had to trim their staffs and intervention services. And overburdened private therapists and referral agents find it more difficult to be paid for interventions.

Earlier intervention is more effective. Those closest to the problem are in the *best* position to spot it and get results because they carry the biggest emotional "hammer." Most of the two million people treated every year were intervened on not by professionals but by concerned others, as desperate "confrontations" with little or no information.

Dare to Confront! is a manual for a nation of volunteers ready and willing to end the drug crisis in their homes and neighborhoods. It describes the best techniques available to motivate those who are chemically dependent to get help.

THE HONORABLE RUTH LEWIS FARKAS, ED.D.

Preface:
Because You Care

◆

What's a nice person like you doing in a book like this? YOU never hoot with the owls all night and slither with the garden slugs in the morning. YOU don't maintain an intimate affair with the WearEver carpet in the hall. And YOU don't boast or blast with the awesome power of Mount St. Helens!

YOU don't believe passion is possession, self-worth is net worth, or viability is "lie" ability. YOU don't recall everyone who ever owed you a nickel while constantly losing your paycheck; miss important tax appointments while drinking over life's disappointments; remember the precise location of a stray can of beer but not where the hell you left the kids. YOU never abuse alcohol or drugs. Everyone depends on you. You're always there.

It's your strength, and weakness, that you care deeply about someone who is out of control. You are probably angry, frustrated, resentful and exhausted. You have two choices: live with it (no problem is so great that it can't get worse) or change it!

You have the power to blow the whistle: get that person's attention, call for help, and launch a full-scale rescue mission! Millions of people seek recovery every year because someone else—family, friend or associate—pushed them into it. Not only can you convince someone to get help—you could be the only person who ever will.

You may hurt more than the dependent. After all, you are not "self-medicating." But once the problem is addressed, everyone involved can begin to heal and grow. By taking the initiative, everyone recovers.

Here you'll discover answers to things you always wanted to know and probably won't hear anywhere else: what is and is not an addiction, its causes, the roads to recovery (expressways, detours and dead ends) and how to make recovery happen. We've attempted to be rigorously honest. You'll learn what you, an ordinary person with little more than a desire to help, can and cannot do.

This book describes community interventions. The techniques presented here are used to make the intervention as safe and effective as possible. But, a word of caution: if the person with the chemical problem tends toward violence, depression or suicide, do not attempt an intervention without professional help from a treatment center, mental health clinic or licensed alcohol and drug counselor.

We know what you feel because we have been there. We've wrestled head on with dependency in the people we care about—in our homes, offices, churches, clubs and organizations. Long ago, we lost loved ones to addiction. Early intervention works.

You are not a fool for enduring it this long. You've tried. But the trying, lying, crying and complying has only led to more abuse. It's time to do something—because there is still time and because you care.

BOB AND DEBORAH

Acknowledgments

♦

We would like to thank the many people without whose knowledge, inspiration and encouragement this book could not be written; especially Vernon Johnson, D.D., who developed the group intervention process and led the call for earlier interventions, Darryl Inaba, Pharm.D., P. J. Mahoney, C.E.A.P., Ernest Kurtz, Ph.D., Bob Kent, M.D., Phil Bromley, Ph.D., John Davis, Ph.D., Paul Steinbroner, A.S.C., Rose Dixon, C.A.D.C., and Cruger Thomas, C.A.D.C.

To the patients at Life Center at Sun Valley, and the many members of the Ketchum (ID) and Ashland (OR) Alcoholics Anonymous, Narcotics Anonymous and Al-Anon groups for sharing their continued experience, strength and hope. To those alcohol and drug professionals from Rogue Valley Serenity Lane (OR), Marworth (PA), the Friary (FL), Hope House (MD), Oakview (MD), Changing Point (MD), the Gateway Centers (FL), New Beginnings (MD), the Walker Center (ID), Serenity Lane (OR), Port of Hope (ID), the Jefferson Employee Assistance Professionals Association, and especially the Life Center at Sun Valley (ID) for their valuable ideas and input over the years.

To the Reverend Charlie and Diane Burger and the St. Thomas Episcopal Church Community, Ketchum (ID), and the Reverend Tom and Margaret Breidenthal and the Trinity Episcopal Church Community, Ashland (OR), who provided friendship, encouragement and prayers. To Deborah's family for helping to support this project in many ways, especially Henry and Sylvia George, Jan and Todd Smith, Ron and Becky, Hank and Seale, Christine, Ken, Greg and Ida, and Dr. Steve and Nancy George, and Jean and Roger Meeks. To our dear and special friends Jim Higgins, Chuck Lawson, Jeanette Clegg, Jim and Julie Romberg, and Shirley and Ken Moser. To our dedicated agent, Denise Marcil, our visionary publisher, Susan Stautberg, and all the wonderful people at MasterMedia Ltd. who believe in us and the importance of this book. We especially thank our children, Bob, Craig, Cindy, Patti, Samarah and Sharolyn, for their optimism, humor, patience and love. You are our greatest blessing.

Introduction:
You're Not Alone

◆

Addiction. No other problem has affected so many American lives so deeply that the President of the United States has called on everyone to get involved—to help the people we know "get off drugs."

To "dare to confront" sounds frightening or even Big Brotherish to most people initially when an intervention is suggested to deal with a loved one's drug or alcohol problem. This reaction stems from a widespread lack of understanding about the impact of addiction on our lives and the lives of the chemically dependent.

This book, masterfully written by Bob and Deborah Wright, effectively attacks these gaps in public knowledge about the addictive process. Then it outlines a strategy for "concerned others" to initiate and perform a successful intervention.

Labeled a worldwide plague on all humanity by the World Health Organization in August 1989, addiction is now very much a global problem with increasing rates of alcoholism, opiate, cocaine, amphetamine, sedative and other drug problems occurring in almost every nation.

Addicts are not comprised of weak, bad, stupid, crazy or indigent individuals. To the contrary, most addicts are among society's most skilled, sensitive and talented individuals. For example, studies have shown higher incidences of addictions among physicians, nurses, psychologists and people with high IQs, as compared with rates for the general population.

Dependency on alcohol and other "legal" addictive drugs results in about 420,000 deaths in the United States annually—about 70 times the number who die from cocaine or heroin addiction.

It is the nature of an addiction to isolate the addict and the family. But if you are a concerned other or if you are an addict, you are most certainly not alone.

Dare to Confront! explains the disease process of addiction and the current theories about how it occurs. This is important because the major symptom of addiction is denial. Indeed, the addict is the least able to recognize his condition until he suffers severe life consequences as a direct result. This denial is extremely powerful and complex. We all tend to avoid issues which cause us pain or discomfort. The realization that one is an alcoholic or addict is extremely painful. The natural tendency to deny is magnified in the addict by the toxic effects of psychoactive drugs on the brain. Alcohol, marijuana, PCP, cocaine and other drugs of abuse impair judgment, diminish cognitive ability and disrupt memory function. Blackouts or amnesia episodes commonly occur in addicts, making it even more difficult for them to recognize the problems they are experiencing.

If the addict cannot intervene in his own dysfunction, then those concerned others who can MUST accept that responsibility.

The most valuable part of this book is the authors' overview of the intervention process and invaluable suggestions on how to deal with resistance. "Part 3: Conducting an Intervention" separates this book from most other books in the field. It teaches the specific skills needed to effectively and appropriately confront those who are suffering from addiction. Here the Wrights address the common pitfalls and gaps that occur during an intervention which can threaten its success. Manipulation, for example, is a major symptom of addictive disease. By being aware and armed with appropriate clinical tools, the intervenors will be better able to neutralize an addict's attempts to manipulate.

Dare to Confront! is written in language that makes sense; is easy to read; and is interesting to follow. It makes effective use of anecdotes and metaphors that are unique to "the recovery field." Utilizing quotes from recovering addicts, the book is interesting and enjoyable to read. I am honored to have been given a chance to introduce it and can think of no other more timely material to address our current addiction crisis. It's about time!

DR. DARRYL S. INABA, PHARM.D.

Darryl S. Inaba, doctor of pharmacology, is director of the Drug Detoxification, Rehabilitation and Aftercare Project of the Haight-Ashbury Free Medical Clinics in San Francisco, associate clinical professor at the University of California Medical Center, San Francisco, and co-author of Uppers, Downers, All Arounders *(Cinemed, 1989).*

DARE
TO
CONFRONT!

IT'S A
PROBLEM!

◆

"We have this problem with Ann. She's always on a roll. I think everyone in the family is too embarrassed or intimidated by her. It's as if there is this 'group guilt' because one of us is imperfect in some way. So everyone hides it. Someone should do something."

"How about you? She's your sister."

"Me? Do I look like Marie Antoinette? I like my neck!"

◆

Someone in your life has a chemical dependency problem. But should YOU be the one to get involved? How do you know it's a problem? How far has it progressed? And what's the prognosis? You'll find the answers you need in the next three chapters.

Had Enough?

◆

"The first thing I noticed was that Joe made a lot of trips to the john. I thought to myself, 'Either he has a weak bladder, a great magazine or a real serious rendezvous with someone I haven't met.' It never occurred to me his lady-in-waiting was 'Snow White.'"

Someone you know has a chemical problem and needs help. He or she isn't sick and tired of the screw-ups, but you certainly are and so is everyone else!

Maybe it's the poor performance, accidents, broken promises, arguments, countless mistakes or sullen children. Or maybe you can't afford the time, energy and patience it takes to keep that "rag doll" of a person together. Every time you pick up the lost arm or leg and stitch it back, it falls off again. You thought your frantic mending and patching helped, but the

3

seams have finally popped and you're left holding a tattered sack of excuses, denials and blame. Enough!

You might be a friend, relative, spouse, parent, son, daughter, employer, employee, co-worker, doctor, client, teammate, minister or any person who cares.

But circumstances have made you dependent on a chemically dependent person. The time has come to change things—for everyone involved.

Tragically, the person you care about doesn't seem to care about you or anyone else. After all, he has put something that can be held in a bottle, capsule, baggie, vial, pipe or syringe before *everything* in life. What's worse, you know it won't get any better.

You say this person may not have a real alcohol or drug dependency.

If you suspect a chemical dependency problem, you are probably right, whether it's abuse, dependency or addiction.

One thing is certain. The wrestling match between human being and chemical has gotten out of hand. It's time for a referee to step in and blow the whistle—expose the problem, call for help and get between the person and the addiction.

Not That Bad Yet?

You say you're "just getting some background information"—that the abuser in your life isn't that bad yet, still lives with the family, holds a job (95% of the chemically dependent do) and appears to function. Maybe he is respected professionally and socially, has never been arrested and doesn't verbally or physically abuse anyone, at least without cause. Maybe she shows no signs of permanent mental and physical damage. And maybe he hasn't seriously hurt or killed anyone—a family member, friend or innocent person—YET! But do you really want to wait for that to happen before you do something?

You say "those kinds of tragedies won't happen in this case." But judges, counselors, social workers and police have found that alcohol and drug abuse is largely responsible for the rampant number of traffic injuries and fatalities, white collar and street crimes, hospitalizations, drownings, fires, assaults, homicides, suicides, divorces, battered women and abused children in our society today. Sadly, each of these chemically induced horrors could have been prevented if someone like you had stepped forward in time.

Regardless of good intentions, promises or positive thinking, when people are chemically dependent, they lose their common sense and good judgment.

Most chemical abusers are not Frankenstein's monsters or werewolves preying upon the innocent. They are people, like you and me. But when they swallow, inhale or infuse a certain compound, they get downright bizarre! They become hideous Mr. Hydes. No matter how much they love us, hate themselves and want to quit, they can't stop taking the crazy chemical. Their behavior gets uglier and uglier, and eventually so do they.

Regardless of their character, upbringing, education or dreams, or how much you believe in them, when they are chemically altered they make mistakes. Unfortunately, most "mistakes" are irreversible.

Whose Responsibility?

You say, "This isn't my responsibility." It may not be your responsibility to protect this person from self-abuse. But it most certainly is your responsibility and the responsibility of anyone else aware of the problem to protect innocent bystanders from permanent mental and physical injury or accidental death. You can't undo a tragedy once it has happened. But you can help prevent it.

It's time for everyone to get involved—beginning in our homes, our workplaces and our communities. You can turn a life around. It works.

How? With a tool called an "intervention." You'll find it is readily learned, easily applied and dramatic in its results.

"Intervention" itself is a confused, often abused word thought by some to mean reprimand, confiscation or a recruitment action taken only by professionals to get a dependent into a specific treatment program. But anyone can intervene toward any purpose. Webster's dictionary best describes an intervention:

"To come between people, things or events as a third party for the purpose of causing a change by compelling an action to alter a condition."

In a chemical abuse intervention, the first party is the

mind-altering chemical. The second party is the abuser. Anyone, including YOU, can be the third party.

All interventions put something between the person and the chemical. The differences in types of interventions are just a matter of "pushiness."

They range from the subtle to the supreme, including: (1) a self-help visit from a recovering person inviting the dependent to a meeting; (2) a threat at home or work; (3) a confrontation by concerned others using enforceable ultimatums; (4) an assertive professional intervention; (5) jail; and (6) untimely death—the ultimate intervenor. You can be involved in the first five and prevent the last.

This book teaches "concerned-other intervention"—an action where family, friends and/or associates confront a chemically dependent person in a loving, caring way and, with evidence of the dependency and enforced ultimatums, convince the person to seek help.

Concerned-other interventions use the very same techniques that professionals have used for over 20 years, and which have worked time and time again in motivating a dependent person to accept help.

Why So Long?

You ask why other people haven't dared to confront earlier. Here are 15 of the most common reasons:

1. Most people prefer begging, pleading or extracting trades or promises. ("Honey, I'll get another job if you'll stop drinking.") Eventually, these all fail.

2. Most people think it requires a professional to effectively confront an addict. ("I wouldn't know what I was doing! I'm not a therapist.")

3. They are afraid of failure. ("They'll blame me when Carl goes out again.")

4. Many prefer the predictable role of a co-dependent, martyr or enabler to the great unknown. Without understanding why, they are reluctant to rock their only boat, no matter how fast it is sinking. ("Sure, Pat parties hard, but that job is so stressful and we really need the money.")

5. Some think professionals or members of self-help

groups will magically appear at the doorstep without being alerted or invited. ("Someone will notice pretty soon and talk to Lois.")

6. Most think it's the job of the outside helpers to take the first step. ("Those people should get Lee into AA. Why don't they say anything?")

7. Most people don't think it's a dependency until a crisis happens. ("John's not that bad, really. Besides, it's not all the time. And he never causes trouble.")

8. People are afraid there will only be one chance at an intervention and they don't want to blow it. ("I'll screw it up and Lou will never want help.")

9. They think an intervention is more difficult than it is. ("What'll I do if Al gets mad?")

10. Some don't want to lose a drinking or using partner. ("We're best friends. Marcie trusts me. I don't want to ruin our friendship.")

11. Some will do anything to keep harmony (or the outward appearance of it). They don't want the unpleasantness of a confrontation. ("You must be kind to your dad. He doesn't mean what he says. He's always sorry. Please don't start another fight.")

12. Most fear there will be some legal or financial repercussion. ("If I say, 'It's me or the coke,' I've lost Mark and a home.")

13. Many don't know how to recognize a dependency before a crisis happens. ("Casey's never had a DUI or passed out at a party. He just forgets things, like where he dropped off the kids.")

14. Some don't want their own drinking or using to come under close scrutiny. ("Look, we all have been blasted at one time or another. Lay off Tyler. None of us are angels.")

15. Most common of all, they don't know how. ("I've tried everything! How do I stop Kate?")

Act Now

This book is written to urge you to take action NOW. You can make a difference. This book will give you the courage and know-how to change the situation closest to you.

It will not teach you how to become a professional interventionist. It *will* show you how to be a volunteer intervenor—someone who can get between the abuser and the drugs.

Whatever the degree of dependency involved, this book will tell you what to say to motivate someone to seek help; show you how to predict what will happen; teach you how to follow through with your ultimatums; and guide you to the best recovery resources available. It is written in plain talk for ordinary people who simply care enough to get involved. Professionals may find the book's visual aids and checklists helpful, as well as gain a unique perspective of a dependent's action style.

It's time to prepare yourself. Your opportunity to confront the person may come when least expected. Sometimes a spontaneous intervention works best, when neither you nor the dependent has time to work up a serious anxiety. For the benefit of everyone involved, you must know what is going on. Contrary to popular belief, getting someone to seek help does not require a professional!

Anyone with enough care and concern can intervene. The only requirement is that you be well prepared—educated, armed and directed.

A Win-Win Situation

Intervention is a win-win situation. If the dependency is in the early stages, the intervention may be enough to cause the person to change. If the disease has progressed and the dependent—in total denial—refuses help, the intervention hasn't failed. You will have ruined the abusing forever because someone has blown the whistle! The chemical dependency has been uncovered! The great charade has ended! The marathon breakdance is over.

Deception is the hallmark of the abuser who cleverly concealed the dependency for so long, structuring all life around it, timing the intake, loading up before and after anyone was around (as if nobody would notice), covering up mistakes, stockpiling excuses, etc. Everyone was fooled, or so the dependent thought. But now, because of your intervention, the wires and mirrors will be exposed. The magic act will be over!

Don't expect this book to be a panacea—a cure-all. Dependency is "cunning, baffling and powerful."

Most addicts would sooner take cyanide than ask for a miracle cure. Sound crazy? It is! But it's just as crazy for you or me to expect rational behavior from a chemically altered mind!

Be realistic. Some interventions do not succeed. There may be another chance, but there are no guarantees. After all, some 30 million practicing addicts have found security in a society of enablers that is too scared, too confused or too selfish to put a stop to it.

Unless a stop to the abuse is forced, unless ultimatums are carried out by you and everyone else, the abuse will continue as long as excuses buy time.

Don't expect immediate, permanent sobriety. Recovery is usually a long process. The "white light" or "burning bush" experience is rare. And, even on the road to recovery, the first step is always the hardest.

Sometimes attempts to help bring ever-greater disappointment as the dependent person continues along a course of downward mobility. For some, all the doors must slam, the bridges flood and the paychecks stop before they cry out for help. Even then, some do not accept recovery. In some cases, family intervention is not possible, due to a history of anger, abuse and denial.

Willing or Not!

The chemically dependent do not need to be willing to be helped. They can be coerced to try abstinence (even if just to get the "heat" off). Fortunately, that is enough of a crack in the door to let the light in, and most people can recover. It is even possible in most states to help people who refuse help. If they are truly life-threatened or endangering others, many states allow court orders for treatment.

Left to itself the disease always gets worse, never better. Regrettably, the addict can't stop and, left alone, will probably die trying. Most do.

If the abuse could be controlled, it would have been before now. How many people do you know who volunteer for a slow and excruciating poisoning?

The stakes are high, but the odds are in your favor. Chemical dependency is the most treatable of all the chronic diseases.

The vast majority of those who accept outside help begin their recovery on the first try. Just by making a start, you are succeeding in ways you may not be able to measure today.

For the abuser, intervention is a dark cloud with a sterling lining. Few things compare with the miracle a person who turns his or her life around to greet each day with honesty, responsibility, gratitude, love and a fervent desire to make up for lost time.

Unsung Heroes

Don't look for credit. People won't applaud you for saving a life from cirrhosis, arrhythmia, accidental homicide, or (as alcoholics say) "the mire of pitiful, incomprehensible demoralization"—not the way they would if you saved the same life from drowning in a duck pond. You may even be resented for rocking the lifeboat, breaking the co-addictive code of silence, or embarrassing the family and friends out of the public "veil of perfection."

Be realistic. No one decorates heroes in the War on Dependency.

The march to recovery takes years; and you, the valiant and courageous bugle-blower responsible for leading the brigade, will be long forgotten by the time a victory is apparent.

A Little Detachment

No matter what your relationship is to the abuser, by offering help you may tend to get emotionally involved in the success or failure of your efforts—it's only human. However, such feelings will work against your effectiveness. Hand-wringing paralyzes the brain and diminishes the ability to stay one synapse ahead of the alert and skittish addict.

There is a point at which you must let go. You cannot control outcomes. You do what is reasonable—then you must let go and leave the results to God. (If you haven't already learned it, you're not Him!).

Addiction professionals and thousands of Al-Anon family members (the "spouses of the souses" and other close family and friends) will readily assert that detached love achieves far greater results than any degree of emotional or ego involvement.

Humor Helps

Intervention is a deadly serious endeavor. It's literally a matter of life or death. But, even in wartime combat, it helps to keep one's perspective by maintaining a sense of humor. Dependency is crazy. It makes us all do bizarre things to compensate. Sometimes we need to laugh. The comic relief comes directly from people in recovery who have developed the admirable ability to laugh at themselves in the face of hell to survive an emotional Armageddon.

The longer the dependency continues, the less the chances of recovery. You are dealing with a chronic and fatal disease. It has always progressed further than the outward evidence shows. Someone needs your help badly and needs it now. Where do you start? You already have by picking up this book and reading this far. The rest will come one step at a time.

Remember, you will never have more impact than you can have right now!!

How Can You Tell If There's Really a Problem?

◆

"Doesn't everyone lose their car? It was a big parking lot!"

"But, Roger, other people eventually find them."

You're probably saying to yourself, "What if I'm overreacting? Maybe it's just the pressure in his life! Maybe I should give it a while longer. Maybe I should leave this mess to others who know more about it. How do I even know if there's really a dependency?"

It's only natural to wonder if you're doing the right thing, especially since people altered by drugs don't grow fangs and long nails to warn us. And whistle-blowing feels more like

13

breaking confidences than breaking the bondage of chemical slavery.

It's also natural to feel guilty and naive when the full picture surfaces, revealing that an intervention should have come much earlier: "How was I so blind? She flashed all the signs in neon red right in front of me for five years! Where was I looking?" If a dependency exists, the evidence is often in plain view, just somewhat camouflaged. Ask yourself:

- Is the abuse affecting any part of his or her life?
- Is this person trying to take control of the universe?
- Is this person all bluff and no stuff?
- Is the abuse affecting any part of your life?
- Is there hard evidence of a dependency?

We will explore these questions later in this chapter.

Who's the Dependent?

You probably think your problem is a certain person who has developed an unhealthy relationship with a chemical. Don't be deceived.

If you depend on a chemically dependent person, YOU have a problem with a chemical dependency! You have become co-dependent.

You cannot address the chemically dependent person in the same way you would a rational person with a reasonable disorder. As long as the chemical is inside the person, you will always be talking to the chemical—not to the person.

Your problem is with the chemical dependency. Your villain is the chemical-in-the-person, not the person. Unless you address the problem on this basis, you will be just another part of the problem instead of a part of the solution.

Chemical dependency is a physical, mental and/or emotional need for a mind-altering substance where continued use takes precedence over family, friends, co-workers, job, health, the law or financial stability.

The real problem is that the chemically dependent person doesn't realize that the problem is the chemical. To the alcoholic, Smirnoffs and olives aren't the cause of the problems— they're the delicious solution to them!

All addicts know something is wrong, but they don't know how to fix it. It's like an auto mechanic who can't make his own car work right, won't ask for help and vainly keeps trying to do the job himself. A surgeon in his right mind would not try to perform brain surgery on himself, but that's what dependents do when they try to control their using.

Cocaine addicts think, "One more line and it'll all come together. I just need a little jolt to stimulate those creative juices. I'm almost there." Alcoholics sit religiously in the front of a bar and order, "Just one more, then I'll have the whole thing figured out."

Whatever else you may learn about chemical dependency, there are five things to remember for any help you offer to be effective: (1) it is a disease; (2) it is progressive—it always gets worse, never better; (3) it is ultimately fatal; (4) it can be arrested; and (5) it is the most treatable of all chronic diseases.

Chemical dependency occurs regardless of whether the substance is purchased on a street corner or from a corner grocery store, prescribed by a doctor or served with dinner, FDA approved or DEA "controlled," manufactured by a pharmaceutical company or by the biochemistry of the human brain, or supports South American drug czars or even the U.S. government through licenses and taxation. Addiction is addiction. It is completely impartial in whom it selects as victims.

Unfortunately, the human body does not care whether or not the substance is legal or socially approved.

This is a brutal, life-and-death subject. Addictions left alone don't magically reverse themselves the way hemorrhoids, ulcers and bad hearts sometimes do. They are progressive, heading in one direction only: an untimely death, or, worse, a torturous, living hell.

The time for family, friends and associates to be "benignly removed" from the chemical crisis in America is over. Abusers in our lives aren't funny anymore. So-called "recreational" drug users aren't a party. They're depressing. And the Andy Capp-like social drinkers floating amicably out of the bars at night aren't comic any longer. They're killers.

Drug Abuse Warning Signs

CATEGORY	DRUG	ABUSE INDICATORS
Stimulants	Amphetamines Phenmetrazine Cocaine*	Hyperalertness, excitation, euphoria, rapid speech, frenzied physical activity, rapid pulse, high blood pressure, insomnia, lost appetite. * The above plus anxiety, egotism, overconfidence, paranoia.
Depressants	Barbiturates Methaqualone Tranquilizers Antihistamines Alcohol*	Drunken behavior (without the smell of alcohol), slurred speech, loss of memory, disorientation, lessened inhibitions, impaired judgement, slowed reaction time, unpredictable behavior. * The above plus smell of alcohol, loss of coordination, impaired distance perception.
Narcotics	Opium/Codeine Heroin Morphine	Euphoria, respiratory depression, drowsiness, constricted pupils, nausea, drunken behavior.
Cannabis	Marijuana THC Hashish	Euphoria, red eyes, fatigue, poor concentration, relaxed inhibitions, craving sweets, disorientation, apathy, poor memory/coordination/ perception of time and space.
Hallucinogens	LSD PCP* Mescaline Mushrooms	Floating euphoria, poor depth perception, visual disturbances, illusions, hallucinations , numbness, speech impairment, loss of memory, poor concentration, a sudden down or crash, dilated pupils.
Inhalants	Solvents Propellants	Laughter, weightlessness, disorientation, loss of motor coordination, impaired vision, memory loss, weight loss, violent behavior.

SIGNS OF WITHDRAWAL	SIGNS OF AN OVERDOSE
Apathy, long periods of sleep, irritability, depression, panic, disorientation, paranoia. *The above plus trembling, terror, suicidal tendencies.	Agitation, high body temperature, paranoia, hallucinations, convulsions, brain damage, death. *The above plus seizures, respiratory arrest, violence, coma.
Anxiety, insomnia, tremors, delirium, convulsions, possible death. * The above plus anger, isolation, unpredictability, panic.	Shallow respiration, dilated pupils, cold clammy skin, weak and rapid pulse, coma, possible death. * The above plus cirrhosis, bleeding esophagus, digestive dysfunction or cancer.
Watery eyes, runny nose, yawning, loss of appetite, irritability, chills, sweating, cramps and nausea.	Shallow respiration, dilated pupils, cold clammy skin, weak and rapid pulse, coma, possible death.
Insomnia, hyperactivity, decreased appetite, extreme mood swings, aggressiveness, panic.	Fatigue, paranoia, possible psychosis, increased heartbeat, hallucinations.
Depression, isolation, temporary schizophrenia, paranoia, aggressive behavior, excitability, incoherence, psychosis-like behavior.	Elongated tripping, permanent brain damage, psychosis, possible death. *The above plus homicidal tendencies.
Depression, lethargy, disorientation, anger.	Bone marrow damage, arrhythmia, death.

Problems in the Abuser's Life

Abusers are like rag dolls that may be cut from the same pattern. But because they differ according to their life experiences, when they fall apart, different seams pop. For one, it might be a lost job, for another a lost custody battle.

Is the abuse affecting any part of the person's life?

Look for popped seams and you'll begin to sniff out a "chemical protagonist" at work. For example, patients in treatment report getting help for different reasons:

"I prided myself on my great physical shape, but suddenly my heart gave me trouble. I knew it was time to get straight."

"My health never suffered, amazingly, but I almost lost my driver's license twice. Finally the judge said, 'You get help or you get roller skates and 60 days.' "

"My partners said I had made $2 million in bad loans in the last five years. Either I go to treatment or they'd call in the notes on my investments. Until that moment, I thought I had held everything together pretty well."

"I still have my job and my money, but my family bolted. Sally filed for divorce and moved to Maryland with our two daughters. I'd gladly give up everything to get them back. The best I can hope for now is visitation rights."

When the Silent Destroyers we call "drugs" throw a life out of balance, it shows up first in one area more than the others. But as the dependency progresses, all aspects of life are affected: mental, emotional, physical, social, occupational, family, legal and financial.

Like a mud slide, the disease develops silently, gradually eroding the very foundation of a person's life before the final, sudden, destructive torrent of addiction puts an end to it all.

Both the dependent and those nearby miss the connection between the substance and the destruction.

Disasters and disruption become such a predictable part of life that the addict expects, accepts and copes with them. Losing car keys and sometimes whole cars or forgetting to pick up the kids becomes an everyday part of a continuing crisis.

When the problems pile up, someone or something else gets the blame. Usually it's the spouse, the kid, the boss, the job or the pressure—never the culprit chemical. Friends and family strengthen the denial by accepting the excuses, assuming responsibility for the addict's frustrations, and coping in their own way without ever confronting the real problem.

When life disintegrates into a tattered mess, and denial and justifications no longer work, the rag doll changes the scene. The "fight" failed, so it's time for full-on "flight." Called a "geographic," the running and gunning chemically dependent person suddenly switches location, believing that where one is causes the problems. But the problems always follow.

The geographic may involve unpredictable disappearances lasting several hours or several days, or a sudden and unannounced change of jobs, households, bed-mates or towns. Eventually, every part of the person's life is a mess. The addict thinks the only way to mollify everything is to physically escape it. But no matter where he goes, it's always "here." The cat can't escape his tail. A geographic almost always indicates that a serious dependency is at large.

Remember that the first clue to a dependency is often that some part of the person's life is falling apart.

No Hiding Hyde

When people finally point their fingers at the real problem ("Sue, you shouldn't take so many pills! It's no wonder you can't concentrate!"), the dependent's first love is threatened. The obvious defense is denial, followed by a string of excuses and justifications.

The addict experiences a critical and compelling need to keep everything in rigid order while denying there is anything amiss.

When the excuses no longer work and the rag doll's world starts falling apart, he suddenly transforms! A monster emerges! The threatened addict takes on the authority of a criminal court magistrate, handing down scrupulous judgments on the shortcomings of others to conceal his own deficiencies.

Is the person trying to take control of the world?

The worse the compulsion, the more the dependent tries to control everyone and everything—whether by manipulating, placating, coercing or seducing. The more he or she attempts to change things, the greater the failure, which leads to a greater counterattempt to control.

To the concerned other, it is frustrating, discouraging, frightening and depressing—a lot like watching a fly struggle desperately to beat down the spider's web until he is most hopelessly entangled.

This urge to control seals the addict's fate. The more she tries, the less she has. Ironically, to overcome the obsession, the dependent has to give up the struggle. In fact, many recovering people avoid relapse by reciting the Serenity Prayer whenever the urge to control threatens to go out of control:

> God, grant me
> Serenity to accept
> the things I cannot change,
> Courage to change
> the things I can,
> and Wisdom to know
> the difference.

Obsessive control and manipulation is a good indicator of an addiction run wild. The more power applied, the less there is.

Empty Egotism

As the dependency progresses, and the compulsion to drink or use goes out of control, the addict loses all self-esteem—a blow softened momentarily while using the drug of choice. To cope with this loss when the chemical isn't around, he falls back on an awesome display of "false pride," acting as if he is the center of the solar system.

Is this person "all bluff and no stuff"?

The insecure addict becomes supremely imaginative, offering megaton solutions to minuscule management dilemmas and presenting elaborate visions of an abundant future to the shell-shocked family. Promises abound as the dependent takes on the role of Great Wizard. Stories materialize to support the illusion—magnificent master plans woven from a scant thread of reality.

Soon the supersalesman begins to believe his or her own

stories. The greater the sense of self-defeat, the greater the egotism in projecting an imaginary success. An egocentric manager doesn't know her place in relation to the world around her, so she brazens it through. She's all bluff and no stuff—a hollow shell of an amazingly empty nut.

After snorting some "blow," the cocaine addict will boast of re-creating the entire world, improving on the design, and doing it in three days! The sheer energy expended behind those wide eyes fools everyone into thinking this person is a power-player, an awesome achiever.

Employers, clients, family and friends fall for the charismatic, frenzied activity, mesmerized by this delightfully charming go-getter—until the promises prove empty. Then they are angry and resentful at being taken for fools. Like the addict, they gullibly mistake motion for action; vertical for horizontal. The ducking and dodging addict jumps up and down furiously but gets nowhere, accelerates to full speed but burns up more rubber than road.

When confronted with this lack of performance, the dependent is shocked and claims he has been "screwed" by people after personal gain. The chemically dependent even projects his own character defects on others—assuming everyone else is hiding something, lying to him, trying to get away with the goodies—tarring everyone else with his own brush. The dependent's defense is often a vicious and highly inappropriate counterattack for the scope of the original criticisms. He blames anyone and anything else for the problem.

The greater the ego display on the outside, the greater the insecurity and moral degradation on the inside. Egotism and false pride are excellent barometers of a runaway dependency.

Affecting Others

If you or anyone else thinks that a person's "use" is a problem, it is. If it has attracted attention, it's a problem—as simple as that! Where there's smoke, something is burning!

Is the abuse affecting any part of your life?

If the person's using is forcing you to cover up the problems, to do additional work or to take on someone else's responsibilities over and over again, it's a problem in your life. If that person's inability to maintain the apartment, to make car payments or to remember errands is making you take on more than your share, it's a problem in your life. The chart in Appendix D will help you see how much the person's dependency is affecting you.

Chemical dependency causes problems. It cannot progress long without causing problems in perception, attitude, performance, judgment and, especially, relationships.

Dependency feeds the problems and the problems feed the dependency.

"I used because coming home was always such a downer."

"So what if I got high after work? You would too if you had to deal with what I had to."

"After I injured my back, I needed something to cope with the pain so I could take care of the kids."

Even if a person first uses a mind-altering chemical just to cope with certain problems, before long the dependency and the problems become inseparable.

Who Pays?

Addiction is expensive, and you are paying for it.

You may not be the one paying for the drugs, but you are surely paying for the dependency in hideous and insidious ways:

1. The dependent's poor behavior is a reflection on your character.

2. His problems handicap your ability to do your work and handle your own responsibilities.

3. Chemical dependency costs you thousands of dollars each year in high health, auto and homeowners insurance, health care costs, security systems, and local, state and federal taxes to cover the increasing cost of police protection, criminal justice, health care and welfare services. (Chemical abuse has been associated with the vast majority of the incidents on the dockets of municipal law enforcement agencies nationwide.)

4. If you are an employer, chemical abuse costs you in high workmen's compensation fees, health and liability coverage,

accidents, absenteeism, mistakes, employee conflicts, larceny, waste, poor performance and decisions, lost opportunities, and benefits costs.

5. It will cost you far more if you or someone you love is a victim in an accident, assault, molestation or burglary induced by a chemical dependency.

If the person is causing problems in your life and you know of a history of a chemical abuse, you have two choices: continue to pay for the dependency in ever-increasing ways or force the person to get help.

Gathering Evidence

No matter how poor the performance or unpredictable the behavior, you'll need hard evidence to back up your actions, convince the person to admit the dependency and protect yourself from liability and criticism.

Is there hard evidence of an addiction?

Any hard evidence is valuable in the intervention. It does not prove dependency, only abuse—reason enough for an intervention.

Remember that we live in a poly-drug culture. Most dependents abuse more than one drug. So don't limit yourself to seeking evidence of one specific chemical. It could throw you off.

A positive drug test is powerful evidence. Some jobs require regular, intermittent drug testing. Police will administer a breathalizer test if there is suspicion of driving or operating dangerous equipment while under the influence. The presence of mind-altering chemicals in the system while on the job is reason enough for an intervention. Some adolescents who have been cited for possession of alcohol or other drugs have contracts where they submit to regular testing as a compromise to jail and a fine. Periodic testing is also a requirement in some rehabilitation programs. Once evidence of abuse is found, testing continues until a person is rehabilitated.

Witnessing the abuse by catching someone in the act is the most powerful evidence, especially a documented account by several witnesses or by someone who saw the person abusing on more than one occasion. It is especially effective if such witnesses are among the intervenors. Also valuable are people who observed unusual behavior even though they did not see the person using. At least they can point to a problem that needs further attention. (For example, drunken behavior may indicate an abuse of a number of drugs other than alcohol—inhalants, methamphetamines and opiates. It may also be due to things other than drugs, like epilepsy.)

Bodily evidence should be professionally examined—such as white powder on the person's nose, lip or cheek; tremors; puncture wounds on the forearm or legs; blackened veins or track marks; unexplained bruises; dilated or constricted pupils; and alcohol on the breath.

Finding the drug hidden in the home, personal belongings, workplace, auto or recreational area provides hard evidence. Some common hiding places for alcohol or other drugs are in the back of desk drawers and file cabinets, in toilet tanks, under mattresses, in hollowed-out books, in envelopes, in briefcases, in spice racks and sugar bowls, in jewelry and makeup containers, or in empty, stacked luggage. (One versatile alcoholic hid his vodka in jars of screws nailed under garage shelves, in ski poles and in the windshield washer tank connected by a hose under the dash.) People don't hide things unless there's something to hide.

Finding the paraphernalia is as incriminating as finding the drug. Syringes or single-edge razor blades aren't used much in your average bathroom. Be alert for pipes, cigarette papers, unmarked or multi-pill-filled prescription bottles, small mirrors, one-foot lengths of elastic or rubber tubing, cut-up straws, empty aerosol cans of hairspray/cooking coating/or solvent, empty containers that smell like solvent or alcohol, or containers where something was burned. In short, anything that looks out of place can clue you to look harder. (An assistant in a treatment center was seen at a party carrying a lighted bong which he later claimed was a decorative piece that he was showing to another person. One year later he admitted himself to the same center for treatment.)

A medical, police or social services report can be sound and convincing evidence of a chemical dependency problem. Medical reports are confidential and disclosure requires a court order (unless the physical exam is required for a particular job where the public is at risk). Police reports are a matter of public record and easily obtained. The very first DUI can indicate a dependency problem. Social services reports are also in the public record. If official reports do not exist yet, don't hesitate to demand them at the first sign of a problem—a traffic accident, personal injury or negligence of children.

If hard evidence is not available, or there is doubt, a professional counselor may help arrange for an assessment and will follow through with you.

Gather as much behavioral and physical (hard) evidence as you can. It will be your strongest ammunition in the intervention.

A Note to Employers

In the absence of hard evidence, employers should never try to diagnose a dependency or accuse an employee of an alcohol or drug problem. They may find themselves on the wrong end of a lawsuit.

An employer must document and cite the change in the employee's performance; let the employee know the conditions for further employment; give the employee a chance to explain the problem and seek help or improve performance on his own; and, if problems continue, send the employee for a professional assessment in accordance with a written, publicized and enforced policy. The problem may not be due to alcohol or drugs. Some illnesses and traumas have been known to cause "drunken" behavior without the use of alcohol or drugs.

Drug Abuse Identification

Drugs vary widely in their effects and side effects. A knowledge of them can help you pinpoint the source of the chemical dependency. The above "Warning Signs" chart gives a basic overview. You'll note that the effects of some drugs are somewhat positive, while the side effects are anything but desirable.

Drugs can be classified as uppers (stimulants and inhalants), downers (depressants and narcotics) and all-arounders (hallucinogens and cannabis). They mimic chemicals produced naturally in the body, and they directly affect the central nervous system.

Drugs cannot create new feelings or sensations. They can

only magnify, intensify and extend the ones that already exist in our brains.

That is why they are so popular. Unfortunately, they work with less precision. The pleasurable sensation is unpredictable, short-lived and requires more and more to achieve the same effect. Eventually, they have no effect or require quantities that pose a toxic threat to the body. They cause devastating mental and physical side effects, including cardiac arrest. And they shut down the body's own ability to produce the original, authentic, enduring, nontoxic and replenishable feelings. They leave a person emotionally destitute.

What If You're Wrong?

Rarely, the problems and the abuse are unrelated. If the person is not addicted, the intervention will force a focus on the real problems while she cools her use. If she isn't chemically dependent, abstinence won't be a problem.

Sometimes there is an underlying psychosis—some psychological disorder which exists apart from the chemical use. In such cases, the person needs a different kind of help that addresses the mental illness and the dependency. A professional counselor can arrange for testing if a psychosis is suspected.

Some people worry about being sued for slander if an intervention is arranged for a person who turns out not to have a dependency.

Three things are necessary to win a slander suit: the accusation must be proven false, there must be malice, and it must be publicized. All three must be present without a shadow of doubt.

In an intervention, you base everything on hard, first-person evidence—the people present tell what they saw (hence the truth). Your intentions are to help the person get help and protect all involved (hence lack of malice). And the only people you involve are those already aware a problem exists (hence lack of publicity).

How Far Has It Progressed?

◆

"I'm a naturally depressed person, and coke just helps me cope the way other people naturally do. I can't seem to get by without it. If it weren't for the depression, I'd never use the stuff. I'm not really addicted."

Stages of Dependency

There are four stages in the dependency progression—all of them stages of use. Not all use is abuse and not all abuse is addiction.

The earlier a dependency is intercepted, the greater the chances for a full recovery.

Although you might be able to identify a person in one of these stages, be cautious about labeling a dependency as "use" or "abuse" rather than addiction, since the disease has always progressed further than the outward signs indicate.

STAGE I: EXPERIMENTATION

The first stage of dependency is experimenting. It happens only once—the first time. After that, "effect" replaces "discovery" as the use motive. Experimentation is usually the result of curiosity, defiance or peer pressure: "Everybody else is doing it, so why not?"

STAGE II: SEEKING A SWING

The second stage is most commonly called use (or, to be physiologically accurate, "abuse"). The chemical worked before, so the person does it again and again whenever he wants to feel different, without regard for the impending physical and psychological results. People refer to this stage as "recreational," although it's no party when the recreation passes into preoccupation.

STAGE III: PREOCCUPATION

The third stage, preoccupation, is what is most often referred to as dependency. The person depends on the drug to cope, to get by, to get up, to come down, to relax, to perform. In this stage the dependent will avoid places where she cannot use, or will use before or after attending public functions. Dependents try to maintain a close proximity to their chemical or its availability. During this phase, people will stop using for a period of time but will always return. "Preoccupation" has the semblance of control, such as in "maintenance" or "social" drinking, but the person is entirely dependent on a supply of the chemical to conduct "normal" life. Nonaddicts don't need dope to cope. Preoccupation is mid-addiction.

STAGE IV: POWERLESSNESS

The final stage of dependency is the hopeless, uncontrollable craving, the driving compulsion and the inability to be able to stop and stay stopped without help, despite all the threats and promises. This is what is most commonly thought of when people refer to "addiction," although, as you have seen, becoming addicted is a process.

Addiction or Dependency?

People tend to separate "dependency" and "addiction," but you'll find we use them almost interchangeably in this book. Along the four-stage path to addiction, where Stage I is Experimenting and Stage II is Seeking a Swing, dependency is most often thought of as Stage III (Preoccupation) and addiction as Stage IV (Powerlessness). Although one term seems less onerous than the other, Stages III and IV are both addiction.

The bottom line is that anyone who is dependent is addicted.

This is important. In the average mind, a "chemically dependent" person has just wandered innocently into the addiction—a victim, while an "addict" is a predator—a "low-life," a killer and a thief.

We see the addict portrayed nightly on TV and recognize him easily by his ruffled hair, rough manner and jumbled clothes. In reality, the addict is also the yuppie attorney with his bourbon in the briefcase, the sexy nurse with her barbiturates to get to sleep, the supermom with her Valium as the kids come home, or the sharply dressed police detective jittery with cocaine. They are all dependency victims. They are also all addicts. The disease and those who push addictive drugs are the real villains.

And we are all enablers. Society perpetuates this dependency. Alcoholism, our number-one national addiction, is healthily nourished by such All-American values as the two-martini lunch, the good old boys watching the game, the high life and happy hour. We defend "The American Right to Get Drunk" as vehemently as abortion and handguns.

Signs of a Dependency

The following will give you a brief picture of the mental, physical and behavioral effects that develop during the later phases of dependency:

Stages of Dependency

Determining the stage of a dependency is risky at best. No two addicts are alike. Most exhibit signs from several stages at once. T hese signs may not indicate a dependency by themselves, butwhen several show up, it is a pattern and a signal

	Early Stage III
MENTAL	Alternately drowsy, frenzied Egocentricity Inability to hold concentration Frequent mood swings
PHYSICAL	Bruises Accidents on/off the job High blood pressure Hangovers Nervous twitching Frequent sick leave Frequent urination
OCCUPATIONAL	Repeated absenteeism (1-2 days) Late arrivals, early departures Power-tripping Frequent mistakes/bad decisions Frequent restroom/coffee breaks Repeated missed deadlines
SOCIAL	Hard "party-ing" with friends Amazing drinking/using capacity Excuses for drinking or using Avoiding places without alcohol Drinking or using before events Occasional binge drinking Stockpiling alcohol and/or drugs
LEGAL\FINANCIAL	Delinquent bills Lost or wasted paychecks Careless spending
FAMILY	Frequent family arguments Neglecting reponsibilities at home Blaming problems on family Entertaining extramarital affair
PROGNOSIS	*Good*–if the person can admit a problem and commit to recovery.

to get a professional assessment. The prognosis depends on how far the disease has progressed, the available care and the ability to accept help. If in doubt, it is better to seek help and find it is not needed than to postpone help until it is too late.

Late Stage III		Stage IV
Chronic fatigue Memory loss Blackouts Confusion over details		Frequent blackouts Disorientation, dizziness Hallucinations Chronic depression, paranoia
Excessive sick leave Sexual problems Gastrointestinal disturbances High accident rate Hand tremors Auto accidents Cold feet		The shakes/cold sweats Impotency/frigidity Passing out Doesn't eat/loses weight Rib fractures Liver/kidney dysfunction Bleeding esophagus
Unauthorized leave Increased absenteeism (2-4 days) Missed appointments Pretending performance Friction with co-workers Hiding alcohol/drugs at work		Chronic absenteeism (1-2 wks) Unscheduled disappearances Altercations with co-workers Drunk or drugged on the job Workplace theft/larceny Threatened or lost job
Belligerent, defiant, antagonistic Unwarranted resentments Attempts to cut down Long list of excuses Denial of problem/refusing help Drinking before/in/after events Erratic/unpredictable behavior		Drinking/using mostly alone Lost control of drinking/using Cutting off anyone who interferes Extraordinary hiding places Reclusive/loner No more excuses Repeated failures to quit
DUI warning or arrest Collection actions Borrowing money from friends		Theft/forgery Legal confrontations or jail Repossessions/foreclosures
Broken promises to stop Evidence of family abuse Separation or divorce All-nighters or geographics		Violent/suicidal Loses home/family Kids caught abusing Kids run away
Fair–if help is obtained immediately, with or without consent.		*Poor*–may be beyond the ability to accept help or be helped.

MENTAL SIGNS

Depressed. Anxious. Resentful. Denies dependency. Avoids facing problems through using. Dramatic mood swings. Changes personality. Loses interest in former interests. Absentminded about important things. Imagines things which never happened. Projects unrealistic outcomes. Misinterprets reality. Loses initiative or persistence. Judgmental. Refuses to accept past. Delusions of importance. Pathological lying. Illogical thinking. Paranoia (there isn't really a master plot behind putting that slow driver ahead of him). Suffers blackouts or memory lapses. Loses track of time. May seem awake, but is not "here." Insomnia. Lethargy. Hallucinations.

BEHAVIORAL SIGNS

Overreacts to criticism. Has a short fuse. Gets in accidents. Uses alone. Develops family, social, legal and employment problems. Eliminates things that get in the way of using. Blames others for problems. Talks about feeling guilty, sorry, remorseful. Breaks promises. Isolates self and avoids friends. Can't stop using when others do. Unpredictable behavior. Inappropriate responses. Drinks or drugs more before showing effects (increased tolerance). Surreptitious about using—sneaks it. Grandiose, aggressive, violent. Drinks or drugs with unsuitable companions. Neglects food. Shakes. Behaves improperly. Geographical getting away from problems. Finally loses tolerance (biological rejection). Tries to manipulate others, change the unchangeable. Argues about drinking/using.

PHYSICAL SIGNS

Ill, impotent/frigid, anemic. Stops menstruation. Suffers rib fractures, bruises, nervous twitching, erratic energy levels, high blood pressure, erratic pulse, sweats, liver damage. Craves sweets or anything that can be quickly metabolized into sugar like junk food. (A recent study of rats showed that they prefer booze over water if they've been fed junk food, but will not with a normal diet.)

Common Misconceptions

Several persistent and dangerous misconceptions manage to prevent us from effectively controlling the chemical dependency epidemic in America today.

A person is only impaired when using. FALSE!
The effects of a chemical on the body can take days or even weeks to wear off physically, while the effects on the mind may take much longer. When the dependent person is not drinking or using, her body is in withdrawal and under extreme stress. She is impaired. Employers used to say, "What you do on your own time is your own business." Now they say, "What you do on your own time affects your productivity on our time directly and dramatically!" When hung over or coming down, the abusing workers, drivers and mothers cannot be very effective when their attention is focused away from their duties and on their plight: how to get more!

A person is an addict only when the addiction becomes apparent. FALSE!
The line of dependency is crossed long before the first withdrawal is visible or experienced. Imagine an iceberg—the size of the tip gives no indication of the tremendous depth underneath. We cannot see into the liver of an alcoholic, for example, to know how far the disease has progressed.

A person is not addicted if they can periodically control their drinking or using. FALSE!
In mid-dependency, a person may unpredictably experience periods of being able to control drinking or using—or even to stop for a while. But inevitably they cannot stay stopped or stop when someone else tells them to.

People with good mental health do not become addicted. Imbalanced people do. FALSE!
Abuse by any "normal" person will eventually produce the biological changes causing addiction. It's a game of Russian roulette—no one knows when their body will kick into the progression, not until it's too late. Mental imbalance is most often the consequence, not the cause of dependency.

Cutting down can lead to cutting out. FALSE!

Cutting down isn't necessary for the person who is not dependent—stopping is no big deal. There is no need to "ease out of it." Cutting down is only an issue for the person who depends on the alcohol or drug. Where dependency exists, cutting down may bring short-term success, but leads rapidly to resumption and an even greater loss of control.

Identifying Progression

The accompanying "Stages of Dependency" chart will help you identify how far the dependency has progressed. Make a check mark next to the characteristics that apply to the person with the problem. No two people are alike, and most will exhibit signs from several phases at once (indicating their progression into the later phases).

While some of the characteristics listed in the chart do not by themselves indicate a dependency, such as being forgetful, divorcing or careless spending, when several occur together, it should be a red flag. Even if the problem proves to be other than a dependency, there is an obvious need to seek help.

A general prognosis is given, based on our experience in working in recovery. But the prognosis for each person is different and depends on the chemical, the person's physical and mental condition, the availability of quality care and the ability of the person to do the necessary work to recover. We have seen several "sure" recoveries fail and many "totally hopeless" ones succeed.

Above all, it is always better to seek help and find it is not needed than to postpone help until it is too late.

Warning: The Volatile Drugs

Some drugs have emerged that are faster, more powerful and longer lasting, causing severe withdrawals, often with extreme violence or depression. Since they addict quickly, people who use them are most likely addicted. While most addiction is to the less powerful drugs, intervention for volatile drugs necessitates taking extra safety precautions and consulting an experienced addictions professional.

Smokable cocaine: crack, freebase, rock, base, hubba, pasta, bazooko. (With marijuana: champagne, caviar, gremmies. With PCP: space basing, whack. With tar heroin: speedball, hot rocks.)

Smokable methamphetamine: ice, crank, crystal, crosstops, cartwheels, whites. (With crack: super crank.)

PCP: krystal, angel dust, hog, peep, ozone. (With marijuana: krystal joint.)

Detoxification

Detoxification should always be medically supervised, especially for the following:

- Sedatives, including sleeping pills and tranquilizers.
- Alcohol if the alcoholic has ever had a seizure, takes "eye openers" or "shooters" or drinks daily.
- Any alcohol or drug abuser with a history of major medical problems including but not limited to heart disease, seizures, insulin diabetes.

WHAT YOU NEED TO KNOW BEFORE YOU DO ANYTHING

◆

"Pat. This is the last time. You promised not to do this to me. If you keep this up, I swear I'll report you!"

"Blow it out your ear, Jack. I don't drink any more than you, and you know it. You're just selling me out for that promotion. I'll stop drinking when you stop."

◆

Before you consider an intervention, you should know a few basics: what causes chemical dependency, what an intervention can do, what happens in recovery, and the resources available to help you.

WHAT YOU NEED
TO KNOW
BEFORE YOU DO
ANYTHING

◆

"Pat. This is the last time. You promised not to do this to me. If you keep this up, I swear I'll report you!"

"Blow it out your ear, Jack. I don't drink any more than you, and you know it. You're just selling me out for that promotion. I'll stop drinking when you stop."

◆

Before you consider an intervention, you should know a few basics: what causes chemical dependency, what an intervention can do, what happens in recovery, and the resources available to help you.

What Causes Chemical Dependency?

◆

"I can't drink alcohol anymore. I've developed this allergy.
Whenever I drink, I break out in spots . . . Las Vegas, Atlantic
City, Reno, New Orleans, Nassau . . ."

Practically since Noah eagerly planted the first vine and
experienced the world's first recorded drunken stupor (wildly
running around naked in his tent, to the horror of his sons),
people have wondered whether the compulsion to drink is a
problem of the mind, the body or the spirit.

Carl Jung called alcoholism "the equivalent of the spiritual
thirst of our being for *wholeness*."

**What really causes dependency? The verdict is not yet in,
but the evidence strongly suggests that mind, body and spirit**

**are all involved at various points in both the progression and
the recovery.**

Most likely, man drinks or uses for a variety of reasons:
mental, physical and spiritual. But he becomes addicted for
biological ones.

Most importantly, he can recover through a mental, physical and spiritual program. In this chapter we will explore the
latest scientific findings.

The biology of addiction is an important phenomenon.
Addicts cannot be helped until they admit powerlessness, and
people by nature are more willing to admit powerlessness over
a physical complication than a mental one. The dependent
acknowledges that he can put down the telephone at will, so he
refuses to believe he can't put down the beer can. He knows he
can't control his diarrhea (his body has a mind of its own) but
denies he needs help to control his chemical compulsion.

Understanding what is known about the biology of addiction can be crucial to helping the dependent understand her
powerlessness, let go of the guilt for a supposed "character
weakness," and accept help now.

Everyone "Uses"

Everyone uses an ample amount of uppers and downers
every day, whether or not we want to or are even aware of it.
We don't have to look very far to find our well-stocked sup-
plier—no further, in fact, than our own brains.

We have our own cache of uppers that energize us, excite
us, make us optimistic and creative, as well as assorted downers
that calm us, make us feel secure, put us to sleep and take away
pain.

Our bodies' natural mind-altering chemicals are called
endogenous, or internally produced, drugs. Some resemble
different types of plugs, each locking into tailor-made sockets.
Others are like little blocking agents that prevent other chemicals (neurotransmitters) from reacting. Externally produced
psychoactives, or exogenous, drugs are able to produce reactions in us by either plugging into the places reserved for our
natural in-body drugs or by effectively blocking our bodies'
natural reactions.

If our bodies weren't already in the mood-altering business, psychoactive drug manufacturers of all kinds would be out of business.

External, or exogenous, drugs include not only the illegal or "recreational" drugs like marijuana and cocaine, but over-the-counter and prescription pain, sleep and stress medications, inhalants like glue and solvents, and all forms of alcohol including wine, beer, hard liquor, mouthwashes and cough syrups.

Reasons for "Use"

People use mind-altering chemicals to change their con-sciousness—to feel, think or sense differently because they are unable or unwilling to accept things as they are instead of the way they would like them to be. Why not? We are a society conditioned against discomfort! Every commercial message promotes a way to feel better, whether it is a cereal to help us move our bowels, a detergent that gives us smooth skin or a shoe that rides as smooth as a luxury car.

Practically from Day One we are advised to rely on a variety of drugs to relieve the discomfort of scrapes, bumps and bruises, toothaches, earaches, backaches, headaches, insomnia, drowsiness, hunger, indigestion, coughs, sneezes, wheezes, burps and gas. We are advised to seek "better living through chemistry."

So when reality is unacceptable and the body's natural painkillers and stress mitigators aren't as fast or effective as desired, we seek external chemical "copers." They may make reality seem more tolerable, but they are certainly not realistic and most definitely are not the panacea they promised to be.

No one sets out to become addicted. People use drugs to feel better, different or happier. But, for some, the use leads to addiction. Why? The psychiatric profession long believed that abuse was a reflection of mental imbalance or "willful miscon-duct." But volumes of new research are indicating that the opposite is more likely true. While people use and abuse for psychological reasons, they crave for biological ones.

Biological Factors: The Allergic Disease

Dependency is often called an "allergic disease" because of the way that the body responds to an addictive chemical. Anyone can become dependent on anything the body rejects. It is the body's natural balancing system, our ability to react and rebound from the things to which we are most sensitive, that sets us up for addiction.

It's easy to think of this biological process as the "one/two" of a knockout in a prize fight. The "one" is a left jab an opponent throws to get a fighter to instinctively dodge to protect himself, but it throws him right into the path of the next punch, the "two."

When an allergen (an alien or threatening substance) enters a sensitive body, the body tries to reject the damaging blow. It sends out an emergency response and compensates.

As an example, a beer makes a normal person feel stimulated momentarily. But it makes the alcohol-sensitive body overreact with excessive stimulant, giving the drinker a real rush or "high." What goes up must come down, and the higher the climb the deeper the crash. The overreaction soon leaves the alcoholic in a dramatic "downer," without the amount of natural stimulant left to carry on normally. Her body is left wide open, defenseless and in need of another pick-me-up. Of course, this is supplied momentarily by more alcohol, soon causing an even greater downer and setting her up for the right-hand knockout punch of a dependency. Each use forces a greater compensation and a greater need.

It may seem contradictory that anyone can become dependent on something the body rejects, but that's exactly what happens. People become addicted to all sorts of things—no matter how initially distasteful they might be, even the first coughing smoke, the first vomited bourbon or the first PCP "bad trip."

Once this adaptation takes place, the out-of-balance system must get more and more, becoming increasingly dependent, because the withdrawal gets worse and worse.

The alcoholic replaces the "bourbon and water" with "bourbon on the rocks," then "bourbon straight up." The average heroin user increases the dose five times within the first month.

Allergists have discovered that people allergic to corn actually crave foods with corn in them! Corn is a common base not only for sugar, margarine and the cooking oil used to fry many junk foods, but for various whiskeys. (Some allergists even go so far as to blame the high number of alcoholic Americans on the predisposition of a corn allergy.)

There is a scale some allergists use which shows how slow or fast substances cause violent allergic reaction and addiction:

Slow: Foods
Oils, fats, proteins, starches, sugars
Moderate: Food/Drug Combinations
Chocolate, tea, coffee, cola, alcoholic beverages, nicotine
Fast: Synthetic Drugs
Glue, solvents, manufactured drugs
Fastest: Natural Drugs
Cocaine, heroin and its derivatives

People can become dependent upon almost anything that causes the body to overreact.

Once the body is hyperreactive to an allergen, it will always be. People deathly allergic to bee stings never naturally develop the natural ability to tolerate them.

People working in recovery point out that dependency on alcohol is always called "alcohol-ISM" and not "alcohol-WASM." Once allergic, always allergic. The only way to stop having a reaction is to cease using the allergen forever.

The question then becomes, "Who becomes allergic and why?" Evidence supports the existence of two types of chemical dependency: one resulting from a biological predisposition and another from abuse.

Biology Determines Psychology

Research over the last 20 years strongly indicates that addiction is the result of complex biological phenomena—not a psychological imbalance. Neurotic behavior is the visible symptom and consequence of dependency more often than the cause. By the time a person craves a drug, his physiology is causing the craving. The mental mess we see on the outside is the result of a biological chain of events inside.

Alcoholics don't abuse alcohol so much as alcohol abuses the alcoholic by changing his physical makeup. This phenomenon is perhaps best described by Katherine Ketcham and Dr. Ann Mueller in their book *Eating Right to Live Sober:*

> [T]he alcoholic in the early stages of his disease experiences changes in his cells that will cause his body to adapt and . . . become efficient at using [alcohol] as an alternate energy source.

Unlike normal drinkers, the alcoholic's liver adapts easily to allow him to metabolize (process) more and more alcohol, thus making him appear to function "normally." In other words, his tolerance increases dramatically beyond that of others. It's an early warning sign that the disease is in progress. Even in the first, invisible stages of alcoholism, his liver can't filter out all the alcohol. Quantities of the poison and the acetaldehyde it produces escape to his brain and play games with his neurotransmitters. The brain cells begin sending and receiving the wrong signals, making him feel like a hockey puck ricocheting all over the rink. He is alternately emotional, reactive, bold, frenzied, paranoid, excited and depressed.

As the drinking increases, it causes uncontrollable mood swings, unpredictable behavior and personality deterioration. It's all due to the chemical reaction of alcohol first on the body and then on the brain.

Most people believe that addiction only begins once some mental disorder appears. But the major biological changes that caused the dependency already occurred when no one noticed anything unusual.

People drink for similar reasons: relaxation, celebration, friendship, stimulation, boredom, etc. But alcoholics gradually rely on alcohol just to "get by." This includes "maintenance" drinkers. They may blame external pressures, but the nuclear reaction inside is already underway. You'll never find nonalcoholics drinking to relieve the pain of not drinking.

Predispositions

There is strong evidence to support the fact that certain people are more susceptible to dependency: the children and grandchildren of alcoholics, those with low production of endorphins, the descendants of certain ethnic groups, those with a natural physical tolerance for alcohol, youth and hypoglycemics.

Finding the exact causes of dependency is difficult because researchers cannot agree on what addiction is and when it occurs. Many studies conflict and, in truth, are more often influenced by the researcher's particular school of thought than objective inquiry.

No matter what the research shows, each person is an individual situation. The addiction and the recovery depend upon a person's specific physical and mental condition and his willingness to accept help.

Hereditary Factors

Like many other diseases, including diabetes, cancer and heart disease, strong evidence exists to show that the precondition for alcoholism can be inherited. It can even skip generations.

Children of alcoholics are four to five times more likely to develop the disease than children of nonalcoholics.

True, the living situation in an alcoholic home is dysfunctional at best. But heredity seems to have a much greater impact than environment.

Children of alcoholics raised from birth by nonalcoholic adoptive parents become alcoholic at a rate three to five times greater than children of nonalcoholics. Sons from broken homes are six times more likely to become alcoholic if the biological parent was alcoholic than if the adoptive parent was alcoholic.

Why do some children of alcoholics become addicted and not others? Is there a gene that can be isolated so we would know which children of alcoholics are susceptible, like we know which babies carry Huntington's disease? Scientists are still looking for the answer. Or, as Dr. Donald Goodwin, the first researcher to establish a link between heredity and alcohol, reports, the answer could be elsewhere: "Environmental factors may determine whether a biological tendency toward alcoholism becomes manifest." Regardless, the hereditary link has been well established worldwide.

Endorphin Research

Curiously, most alcoholics recall their first drink in detail! You'll often hear them say, "I was in pain all my life, but my first drink made the pain go away!" or "Alcohol made me feel whole for the first time!"

A part of the explanation may be found in the endorphin research reported in the medical journals. Apparently not only alcoholics (drinking and abstinent) but the nondrinking children of alcoholics seem to have a lower than normal stockpile of natural "satisfiers" (called endorphins) and therefore a lower than normal threshold of pain. This condition presents a perfect opportunity to seek external "copers" when internal "copers" fail to do the job.

It is entirely likely that alcohol supplies an essential ingredient missing in the brains of many alcoholics, something most people have naturally: internal tranquilizers to cope with pain and stress.

Some of these external copers actually mix with substances in the brain and create entirely new chemicals. For example, some studies show that alcohol acts on chemicals in the body to form what may be the most addictive drug known to medical science! These compounds, called tetrahydroisoquinolines (TIQ's), immediately act on the brain. They are so powerful as to make rodents bred with an aversion to alcohol drink heavily despite their programming.

Externally generated copers (drugs) plug into the sockets made for the internal ones or alter the balancing mechanism of the brain. Unfortunately, they are not as efficient. It takes more and more of them to dull the pain, address the stress or achieve pleasure. Moreover, the more the addict relies on external copers, the more the natural coper-producing mechanism in the brain shuts down. Soon the person becomes completely dependent on the external copers. The result is a chemical dependency on the externally generated copers—addiction!

Ethnic Susceptibility

Although controversial, several studies show that an increased incidence of alcohol addiction occurs in persons of certain ethnic cultures: notably northern European and American Indian. On some Indian reservations in the Northwest, as many as nine of every ten adults reportedly suffer from alcoholism. An unusually high rate of alcoholism also can be found among certain northern Europeans, most notably the Irish, Swedes, Danes and Russians.

Many fewer alcoholics are found among the Mediterraneans, for example the Semites, Greeks and Italians. There are somewhat more alcoholics in northern Italy than southern Italy, despite almost identical per capita consumption and social customs. The limited occurrence of addiction in Mediterraneans seems to persist among their descendants.

Some explanations have to do with drinking behavior, biological makeup, social customs and adaptation over time. But how much of which is unknown.

The French, who have higher rates of alcoholism than Italians, drink between meals, while the Italians drink with meals. Pasta, like any carbohydrate, lessens the effects of the alcohol on the body.

Orientals, who have lower biological tolerance and display an unusual natural aversion to alcohol—flushing and getting ill after two or so drinks—have lower than average rates of alcoholism.

Social customs also appear to have some effect on alcoholism. For example, Jews drink with rituals and celebrations. Heavy drinking is frowned on by Jewish people of all nationalities. They rarely become alcoholic. But drinking is seen as a part of wholesome conviviality in Irish communities. Some societies drink alcohol as if consuming water will cause rust.

It is entirely possible that social customs support a biological need or craving for heavy drinking rather than the heavy drinking being an outgrowth of social customs. (The chicken or the egg?)

Tracking ethnic susceptibility is difficult because of: (1) disagreement on a universally accepted definition of alcoholism, (2) the invisibility of mid-stage alcoholism, (3) the inability of alcoholics to report accurately on their condition due to denial, (4) a lack of resources and mechanisms for long-term quantifiable research, (5) the need to separate out the heredity factor, and (6) government conflicts of interest.

In other words, in most countries of the world, the government is not only responsible for treating dependency, but for producing and distributing alcohol as well as funding and conducting the research. It's a lot like having Dracula guard the blood bank.

For example, few treatment programs can be found in certain countries that manufacture, consume and export large amounts of alcohol. At international conferences they claim to have no alcoholism problem. Meanwhile, their government hospitals bulge with patients seeking help for the addiction-related physical and mental disorders.

Hypoglycemia

By its nature, hypoglycemia may create a biological predisposition for alcoholism. Hypoglycemia, or low blood sugar, is an underproduction of sugars—the opposite of diabetes.

The human body needs a balanced level of sugar in the blood to live. This sugar provides energy in the form of calories. Anything a person ingests can be converted to sugar and then to energy. Complex carbohydrates, like pasta and starches, take longer to be converted, so the energy level doesn't jump so rapidly. But the faster-working, purer, refined sugars process quickly. Sudden floods of sugar register an emergency in the body and generate a "sugar rush" or "high" that can quickly change mood (an effect that varies in different people).

Unfortunately, the sugar high is always followed by a dramatic drop in energy and mood (the "sugar blues"), needing a greater surge of energy to get back up to normal.

Hypoglycemic people can easily develop sugar dependencies—the problem of compulsive overeaters.

The sugar high-low parallels an alcohol high-low because both raise and lower blood sugar. In fact, alcohol *is* sugar—one of the purest and quickest forms to infiltrate the blood, thence the brain. It is not surprising that compulsive overeating and alcoholism tend to run in the same families. As many as 65% of women with eating disorders have either alcoholic parents or grandparents. Two-thirds of women in treatment for alcoholism also have eating disorders.

For obvious reasons hypoglycemia (a sugar deficiency) is a perfect set-up for the high-low scenario of dependency. One study shows 93% of recovering alcoholics to be hypoglycemic.

Part of the difficulty in testing for hypoglycemia is that the signs are difficult to spot, and accurate tests are expensive and time consuming.

Common sense says that if there's not enough sugar in the blood, a person will seek more sugar as quickly as possible. Alcohol is an excellent satisfier.

Differences in Tolerance

For some unknown reason, many people are seemingly born with an inability to tolerate even moderate amounts of alcohol without experiencing unpleasant side effects (headache, dizziness, nausea). They have a natural aversion. Because they tend to limit their intake of alcohol, alcoholism does not occur as frequently among them. Conversely, those who have a naturally high tolerance for alcohol seem to be more predisposed to develop alcoholism. The low-tolerance phenomenon is more prevalent in women than in men and may account for the somewhat lower rate of addiction among women.

New research indicates that those women who do drink socially are at greater risk than men to develop dependency. Not only are their livers smaller, but women lack an ample supply of dehydrogenase, a protective stomach enzyme that breaks the alcohol down and lessens its effect on the body. Alcoholics produce less of the enzyme than social drinkers do. Nonalcoholic women produce 30% less then nonalcoholic men, and alcoholic women produce virtually none of the enzyme.

Differences in Age

People who begin to drink and use drugs in their youth are at a greater risk to develop dependency than people who start drinking and using when they are older.

Because of their smaller size, smaller livers, rapid metabolism and the dramatic growth in both their bodies and their brains, addiction among young people to all categories of mind-altering drugs occurs at lightning speed.

Marijuana research using rats of different ages shows that the young rats sustain more severe brain damage than older rats exposed to far greater amounts.

Young people abuse alcohol six to one over other drugs. Because of their ready access to an unlimited supply (that of family and friends and its availability in grocery store products), alcohol addiction in young people occurs early, easily and with greater severity.

Social Drinking

As many addicts will attest, addiction does not require a genetic, ethnic or biological predisposition.

Anyone can develop a dependency to alcohol or other drugs through a pattern of consistent abuse.

As previously shown, the body's natural copers shut down with consistent use of externally generated copers. The brain actually prefers these false copers and eventually sees no reason to produce the natural internal copers it no longer uses. Because the external copers are not as effective, the brain requires more and more to achieve the same result. Soon dependency results. Hence, over time, moderate social drinking can lead to alcoholism.

Effect on Brain Membranes

Some studies using complex scientific models may help explain how "using" can lead to "abusing." Theoretically, brain cells are coated with a protective membrane. Regular drinking makes the membrane liquefy, then harden, increasing in thickness with each drinking session. The membrane blocks the protein nutrients and the communication between cells. The more alcohol consumed, the thicker the membrane, the fewer the nutrients that reach the brain cells and the more difficult the transmission. The same blocking is caused by things like age, some foods, diet pills and certain drugs.

This theory could explain the blinding flash of brilliance that an alcoholic experiences when drinking. His thinking clears for an instant because a solvent momentarily softens the membranes, briefly permitting his brain cells to communicate better.

Psychological and Behavioral Factors

Most addicts will variously exhibit paranoia, schizophrenia, periodic memory loss (blackouts), unwarranted mood swings, distorted views of the truth, concealments, double lives, talking to themselves, hearing voices, uncontrollable anger, poor concentration, erratic standards (lax and judgmental), extraordinary phobias, and hallucinations—all usually considered indications of a chronic psychosis. The phenomenon is called "addiction psychosis."

The difference is that most addicts are not psychotic—a mind-altering chemical makes them behave that way.

Psychological tests administered before, during and after treatment show that nine out of ten addicts are not psychotic. They may be extremely neurotic, but once the chemical is removed and a program of responsible living is substituted, their mental disorders leave. Such recovering addicts prove to be as mentally healthy as normal people, some more so.

Addiction psychosis often does not appear until the latter stages of the dependency. In the early stages, the dependent appears to function somewhat normally. The cocaine addict seems stable and in control right after some blow. The alcoholic steadies his nerves with a drink. The hash addict is cooperative and supportive after a hit. However, once the addict stops using, erratic and unwarranted behavior signifies that a withdrawal is in progress. It is very common to hear the spouse of an addict in withdrawal claim to like the addict better drunk or drugged.

The dependent will convince others that it's the social pressures and the stress that cause the using. There's stress, all right—the stress to resupply the addictive chemical.

To the addict, the complications of withdrawal are incomprehensibly worse than those of using.

Addiction isn't a state of mind, but of body. The mental disorders will continue as long as the chemical is present. Total abstinence is necessary, along with a new way of thinking, acting and coping. Only then can mental health return.

Willful Misconduct

That a chemical has altered the mind sounds simple, but many educated minds overlook the facts. The mind is falsely considered the battleground on which the recovery struggle will be won or lost. The body is supposed to be a willing listener of what the mind tells it to do, when in fact, just the opposite occurs. The condition of the body preconditions the mind.

We Americans seem to glorify mental strength, from the "Power of Positive Thinking" to "Dianetics," from personal power to self-hypnosis, visualizations and affirmations. We regard with disdain the person who cannot control himself and blame the dependent for becoming addicted in the first place. ("After all, we faced the same problems he did and we did not become addicted. He asked for trouble. He deserves what he gets.")

Addiction is not a matter of willful misconduct. Although there is plenty of misconduct, there is nothing willful about addiction. Willpower has about as much effect on the overpowering compulsion to drink or use as it does on a runny nose.

The popular attitude that the addict shows no self-control becomes a self-fulfilling prophecy. He keeps trying to control the uncontrollable so as not to admit his own failure. Imagine the effect on cancer patients if society regarded them as "failures" at curing their cancer without help. In treatment, addicts are shocked to learn they are physically ill and not hopeless misfits. When treatment is approached from a biological standpoint, the response is positive, assured, committed. The therapists can concentrate on the disease instead of firefighting the dragon guilt. For the most part:

Dependents are sick people who need to get well, not bad people who need to get better.

There will be no victory over addiction in America until everyone realizes that no dependency ever happened as the result of "willful misconduct." This is as ridiculous as saying that someone who contracts lung cancer from smoking did so to commit suicide.

Poor Moral Character

Some people think that addiction is the result of loose morals. But the studies show that the loose morals are a result of addiction rather than the other way around. There are mass murderers who drank and never become addicted, and war heroes who drank and ended up dying in detox wards.

Regardless of moral or ethical standards, there's only one guaranteed safeguard against addiction: if you don't drink, you can't get alcoholism; if you don't use, you can't become addicted.

When a person becomes addicted, morality and ethics DO go out the window. Behavior IS changed. Addicts DO display insufferable antisocial behaviors, but it is the chemical-in-the-person doing the acting and talking. The drug becomes the god, the only thing in the addict's life—all else takes second place, including conscience, family, standards, morality and the law, if they stand in the way of the needed drugs.

Accountability for One's Actions

People should always be held accountable for their actions. This, in fact, is a basic part of the Alcoholics Anonymous program of recovery: to take a moral inventory and to make amends for wrongdoing. It is also a crucial part of the "reality therapy" approach to behavioral counseling. But punishment without rehabilitation and recovery is no deterrent to continued craving and further misbehavior.

Once the addiction is treated, the person's character (morality, ethics, conscience, etc.) returns.

People who work a program of recovery are many times more responsible, considerate and honest than the majority who never had a chemical dependency. They have to be! They've been forced to lead lives of accountability. The only alternative is a slow and tortuous death and the loss of everything they value.

Emotional Immaturity

A common phenomenon of dependency is that it stunts emotional growth. Chemicals that alter, dull or override feelings inhibit healthy emotional growth and development. A 30-year-old person who became dependent at 16 will display the same emotional maturity as a 16-year-old, because that is where the maturing stopped. Once in recovery, emotional maturity develops at the rate that the recovering person is able to deal honestly and openly with feelings.

Extent of Addiction

New national surveys report that as many as 15% of Americans are chemically dependent. Since the physiological changes of chemical dependency occur before the physical or behavioral evidence, long before the abuser is aware he or she has a problem, the actual number is probably much higher. One researcher once said, "If you think there are a lot of chemically dependent people around, multiply by two and you'll probably come closer to the facts."

Susceptibility to addiction, whether by heredity, ethnicity, biology or abuse, is a biologic Molotov cocktail waiting for the match of a mind-altering chemical.

Chemical dependency, if not arrested, is always fatal. Unfortunately, it is rarely cited on death certificates. Instead, you'll see heart failure, accidental drowning, fire, fall, intestinal cancer, aneurism, a gunshot wound to the chest or a massive head injury from hitting a bridge abutment.

"Alcohol" vs. "Drugs"

You'll find that this book treats alcohol and other addictive drugs the same. So does the human brain. Both are psychoactives. They follow the same pathway to dependency. And they ultimately result in mental and physical dysfunction, loss of family, friends, job, belongings, health, freedom and life.

Most importantly, the same recovery program works for alcohol and all other addictive drugs.

Nothing is more misleading than the reference to "alcohol or drug" addiction, as if there were a difference, or to hear alcoholics boast that they are not as bad as other drug addicts.

Alcohol causes the vast majority of addictions worldwide, kills many more people than all other drugs combined and is so potent that, if discovered today, it would be classified as a Class II drug, available only by prescription.

Research demonstrates how alcohol and other drug dependencies have much more in common than just their effects and their treatment. They seem to share the same brain chemistry. For example, the TIQ's produced when alcohol breaks down in the brain are precursors to the production of morphine!

As far as the brain is concerned, alcohol is just a cruder form of heroin or morphine, but a narcotic just the same.

Once addicted to one mood-altering chemical, a person can quickly develop dependence on another. As many as eight out of every ten people in treatment today are addicted to more than one substance, usually to alcohol and a prescription or illicit drug. The phenomenon, known as cross-addiction, is why recovering people must stay away from all mood-altering substances, including alcohol, prescription pain killers and sedatives.

Classes of Addiction

Dependencies range from mild to extreme, but "class" distinctions are dangerous for several reasons: (1) the disease has always progressed further than it appears, (2) substitution of supposedly "less onerous" mind-altering chemicals to treat addiction has failed and, in the end, dangerously postpones help (Valium for alcoholism, methadone for heroin, etc.), (3) addiction to a legal substance is as lethal as addiction to an illegal one, and (4) offering categories of "sickness" gives addicts a welcome opportunity to postpone help and works against all parties involved.

We strongly recommend intervention at any stage of abuse for any mind-altering substance.

If the person can stop on his or her own, good. If not, everything possible must be done to motivate the person to accept outside help immediately.

Addiction is addiction—whether to beer or heroin. A duck by any other name still has webbed feet. Once a person is addicted in any way to a mind-altering chemical, the only way out is total abstinence.

Experimentation, Use, Abuse or Addiction?

People often ask when experimentation ends and addiction occurs. They get all tangled up in what is legal or socially acceptable. The following distinctions can eliminate any confusion:

The first time is experimentation. The second time is use. Use becomes abuse once there is any physical or mental damage to the body that consumes it. Addiction occurs when the person becomes dependent on the chemical to cope with life.

What Is an
Intervention?

◆

"To sober him up, I pumped him full of hot coffee. All I got was a wide-awake drunk."

Now you know what dependency is and that you must do something about it. The next question is "What exactly should you do?" The answer is simply to *intervene*—to jump-start the recovery!

Intervention is a caring and forceful confrontation to convince a chemically dependent person to get help.

The operatives here are "care" and "force," or, more emphatically, "tough love." If either element is missing, the care or the force, the intervention will most certainly fail.

The care—the intervenor's sense of love and concern—addresses the person, gets his attention to really listen and want to hear what you have to say. The care proves that you are doing this for him as much as yourself. The force addresses the disease, realizing that the rational decision to get help cannot be left entirely up to a chemically altered mind.

An intervention may involve one or many persons. The exact structure of an intervention is determined by its objective. Form follows function.

What is it you hope to achieve? If all you want is to get the addict to exercise more self-control, then prepare yourself for failure and all the crises that will follow. Self-control alone doesn't work, even when the addicted person is threatened with the reality of prison or the loss of job, family, home and possessions. Punishment is no deterrent to the craving for an addictive chemical.

There are three types of intervention: professional, mutual aid group and concerned-other. They offer different advantages.

Professional Intervention

Professional intervention occurs when a professional is sought for help to confront the addict. The professional may be a trained interventionist from an alcohol and drug treatment center or hospital, an independent counselor (consultant, psychologist or social worker) or a personnel administrator or employee assistance officer in the workplace.

Professional interventions are formal and organized. The professional leads the intervention and handles the structuring.

If the objective is to get the addict to seek formal in- or outpatient treatment or independent counseling, you may want to consider a formal intervention through the service involved—since the professional interventionist will be following through with the addict. Some interventionists offer their services without charge, with the fee included in the cost of treatment or as a subsidized community service.

In the professional intervention, a counselor confronts the person privately or arranges for family members, employers, friends and associates to confront the addict as a group.

They get together in advance, share information about the person, evaluate the nature and extent of the dependency, decide whether an intervention is needed and, if so, are instructed in how the intervention will proceed.

A specific time and place is arranged for the intervention. The dependent is brought into the room, and each participant honestly and compassionately presents evidence of the person's behavior, as well as personal feelings and concerns. The dependent is offered the opportunity for treatment and usually given an ultimatum from the family, employer, etc. Financial details are usually worked out in advance so that the addict has little excuse to delay a commitment to get help.

OBJECTIVE

Supervised therapy by persons knowledgeable about chemical dependency to give the dependent the best professional help to quit using.

ADVANTAGES

1. The person leading the intervention has done it many times before and is prepared for every type of response from the addict.

2. It requires somewhat less preparation on your part, although it is still necessary to gather background information and contact family, friends and associates to participate in the intervention.

3. Professional interventions almost always work to get the person into formal care.

4. Professional care is supervised.

5. With professional care, the person will get the full attention of people knowledgeable about that dependency and a program of care that has worked for countless others in the same situation.

6. Professional interventionists can help the addict get in touch with financial resources that might be available to help pay for the care.

CONSIDERATIONS

1. Some people hesitate because they feel the dependent may prefer a different place of care than the one represented by

the interventionist. (Fine! The interventionist will handle the arrangements.)

2. Some people will often wait too long before calling in the professionals, until evidence of addiction is overwhelming and the person is too far along to accept help. (Don't wait!)

3. Many people do not have access to professional interventionists because of their geographical location, the workload of the available interventionists or the waiting lists for available treatment programs.

4. Fewer intervention services may be available due to cutbacks in insurance payments to treatment centers, reduced staffs at independent centers and difficulties in compensating independent counselors for interventions.

5. Many times, people cannot afford professional care (which ranges from $35 to $100 an hour for counseling and $5,000 to $20,000 for treatment), especially when insurance policies do not cover the cost and the dependent has long eroded his financial base. (Review the insurance coverage and discuss finances with the interventionist.)

6. Although subsidized treatment programs are available for people without insurance and who otherwise cannot afford treatment, the waiting lists are often three to twelve weeks long. Arrangements must be made by the dependent well in advance. Because the staff-load is high and the waiting list long, many of these services do not offer professional interventions.

7. Many people harbor a deep-seated fear of hospitals and will refuse any type of medical care.

8. No treatment program can guarantee results and some people do not recover even with the best professional care. Recovery depends on the addict's desire and condition.

If professional care is the objective, take the initiative to explore the variety and quality of professional services available as well as the financial condition of the addict and sources of possible assistance.

A good place to start is the Yellow Pages directory of your local or metropolitan phone book. Check listings under the categories: Alcoholism Treatment, Alcohol and Drug Treatment, Drug Abuse Information and Treatment, Counselors:

Alcohol and Drug, Hospitals. Call, ask questions, get written information and visit them. Inquire about licensing, fee schedules, insurance coverage, financial aid, etc.

PROFESSIONAL INTERVENTION

Always consult a professional alcohol and drug counselor before attempting an intervention in the following situations:

- When the person has demonstrated tendencies toward violence, depression or suicide.
- When you or others have been physically threatened by the dependent.
- When there is no one else but you to do the intervention.
- Whenever you have questions or concerns.

The next two types of intervention involve nonprofessionals (or intervenors).

Mutual Aid Group Intervention

The second type, the mutual aid, self-help or "soft" intervention, is led by a person or persons who suffer from the same chemical dependency and are recovering through a program helping themselves.

They call on the dependent person by themselves during or soon after a period of abuse. They listen to the person's "complaints, resentments and justifications" and share their experience, strength and hope. They talk openly about their dependency, carry the message of their recovery and invite the person to come to a meeting. The objective of the intervenors is to keep themselves straight and sober by continually reaching out to others who are addicted. In this way they can remember where they came from, get their minds off themselves, be grateful for their progress and offer it as a source of hope for others.

Mutual aid interventions often happen spontaneously when a recovering alcoholic or drug addict finds himself alone with someone who has a dependency and needs help. The recovering person offers his experience only if the individual wants to hear it.

Such intervention is called "soft" because there is no obligation, no pressure and no ultimatum. The decision to participate is left entirely with the dependent. Mutual aid organizations do not promote themselves but rely on the first-person stories of the recovering members to attract others to join.

The leading recovery program for addiction, Alcoholics Anonymous, was started as a result of a mutual aid intervention. A recovering alcoholic financial analyst who wanted and needed to reach out to other alcoholics was invited by a third party—a nonalcoholic—to speak to an unwilling alcoholic physician.

AA and the groups more or less modeled after it are called 12-step groups because they follow 12 steps to recovery. This type of intervention, "reaching out to the person who still suffers," is a part of AA's suggested program of recovery and is, in fact, the organization's 12th step. For this reason, it is known as a "12th step call."

OBJECTIVE

Recovery through participation in a self-help program that uses the experience of others recovering from the same dependency to help members stay straight and sober.

ADVANTAGES

1. The people intervening have the best experience of all: They've been there before and can talk to the addict in his language, at her level.

2. Mutual aid groups offer addicts the clearest visible proof that recovery is possible.

3. Mutual aid programs allow the addicts a chance to shape their recovery.

4. In mutual aid groups, recovering people find the genuine care and commitment of others with common experiences.

5. The 12-step groups are so successful in supporting recovery that the majority of successful professional treatment programs include them in their recovery plan.

6. They offer a virtually limitless source of lifetime support.

7. Members of mutual aid groups do not charge for their services and readily will offer their time and energy or locate someone else in the program who can help.

8. Wherever they travel, almost anywhere in the world, recovering people can find a 12-step group. Literally thousands of meetings go on every day.

9. The addict knows that the people intervening have no financial interest in his recovery. In reality, they are helping others in order to help themselves stay clean and sober.

10. The only requirement for membership in a self-help group is a desire to stop using the addictive chemical.

CONSIDERATIONS

1. Some practicing addicts will fight help from a 12-step program because they consider it to be for the totally hopeless. (In fact, such programs include people in all phases of addiction and recovery, as well as people of every social and professional status.)

2. Most addicts have become recluses and balk at first at the idea of a group experience.

3. Some people need a more intensive form of therapy offered in a clinical setting.

4. Twelve-step programs are unsupervised and the recovering person must independently commit to work the program and attend meetings to get well.

5. Although many 12-steppers regularly visit shelters, prisons and detox centers to make 12-step calls and will respond to an addict's call for help, they may not be willing to make an unsolicited call at the request of a third party which would put them in an adversarial position.

6. The soft intervention may not be strong enough to get the person to commit to help.

AA and NA groups usually operate 24-hour answering services to speak with the addict and provide information. The number can be found in the White Pages of your local phone book and sometimes in the Yellow Pages under "Alcoholism Information" or "Alcohol and Drug Services."

It is worth the effort to seek out the assistance of a self-help group, especially if the addict has friends or acquaintances who have recovered through the group who are willing and available to call on him.

Concerned-Other Intervention

The third type of intervention can be conducted by anyone who cares.

Called the concerned-other or community intervention, it involves ordinary people coming together in a loving, caring way, to confront and convince the dependent person to get help now.

The intervenor is usually a family member, friend, business associate or minister. If you choose to do it yourself (and there's no good reason why you shouldn't), the intervenor is you!

The vast majority of the two million people who seek professional care each year do so because of a concerned-other intervention.

Most follow a format designed originally by Dr. Vernon Johnson of the Johnson Institute.

The approach is a serious "we love you but you must do something now" type of thing. It is informal and usually semi- or unstructured. It may be planned for a certain time or place, or occur spontaneously when an opportune moment presents itself.

In a concerned-other intervention, one or more persons who know the addict confront the person with hard evidence of the dependency.

Usually the intervention follows a generic theme: We are here because we care, you have a problem, here is the evidence and how we feel, this is a disease and you need help, we cannot accept your behavior any longer, and here are your options.

OBJECTIVE

To get the person to quit drinking and/or using and to seek help.

ADVANTAGES

1. The person leading the intervention knows the addict intimately.

2. It can be effective in the earliest stages (misuse/abuse) of dependency—before a serious addiction is evidenced that would warrant the attention of a professional service or a 12-step group.

3. The intervention can take place anywhere, any time, whenever the best opportunity presents itself, usually at the moment of a crisis.

4. It is flexible. It can be more intimate or more public, depending on what will work best.

5. The intervention can follow whatever course is most appropriate for the person involved.

6. The addict will know that the intervention is done by people out of their care and concern rather than for pay.

7. There is no needless delay due to the lack of availability of a professional.

8. If the intervention doesn't work, it can be followed up by a professional or 12-step intervention or another concerned-other intervention.

9. It costs nothing but your time, concern and preparation.

10. Concerned-other interventions involve the people closest to the dependent not only in the confrontation, but in the recovery, thereby supporting the recovery and extending the benefits to all who become involved in the therapy.

CONSIDERATIONS

1. Time and effort are needed to gather together the information, evidence and other participants.

2. It requires that you learn something about chemical dependency, its effects and its treatment.

3. There are no guarantees that it will result in a recovery. You can only do so much.

4. You will bear the blame as well as credit for daring to confront.

5. Some family and friends may be too angry, afraid or sick (it is a family disorder) to participate without professional assistance.

6. The people intervening are often the same people who have been manipulated by the dependent all along. Therefore they must be alert and forceful to avoid being manipulated during the intervention.

7. You must carry out any and all ultimatums you give.

The only requirement for a concerned-other intervention to be effective is that you be well prepared—educated, armed and directed.

This book teaches how to conduct a nonprofessional, concerned-other (community-style) intervention, but it contains helpful information for more effective mutual aid and professional interventions as well.

Is nonprofessional intervention safe?

Thousands of concerned-other interventions, like the ones described here, are conducted every year by professionals and nonprofessionals alike. While intervention has been shown to be the safest and surest way to stop a dependency and start a recovery, intervening on a chemically dependent person is no more and no less safe than living, working or socializing with that person. The best way to protect everyone is to motivate the person to stop using and get help. You can do so as safely as possible by following the careful instructions given in this book and taking the same precautions that professionals take:

- Never intervene alone.
- Never intervene on the dependent's turf.
- Always communicate care and concern.
- Never place yourself at unnecessary risk.
- If the dependent has physically threatened you or others, remove yourself from danger and notify the police.
- Do not intervene on a person who has demonstrated tendencies toward violence, depression or suicide without professional help.
- Whenever in doubt, call a professional counselor, interventionist or a treatment center for guidance.

SUICIDE WARNING SIGNS

Contact a counselor and do not intervene without professional help if you discover any of the following:

1. Suicide attempt.
2. Preoccupation with death in talk or pastimes.

3. Suicidal gestures.
4. Exaggerated risk-taking.
5. Preoccupation with state of health.
6. Suicide in family history.
7. Evidence of leave-taking (notes about suicide, will-writing or giving away possessions).

6

What Is Recovery?

♦

Two widows stood quietly in the graveyard. One turned to the other and said, "Stroke took mine. What about yours?" The other one answered, "His liver gave out." The first one shook her head. "Didn't he try AA?" "Oh, no," the second replied. "He wasn't ever that bad."

This book has one goal: RECOVERY. And you have only one purpose in reading it: to help someone you care about recover from an insidious and ultimately fatal disease. But what exactly is recovery?

Remember what you have learned about chemical dependency: (1) it is a disease; (2) it is progressive—it always gets worse, never better; (3) it is ultimately fatal; (4) it can be arrested; and (5) it is the most treatable of all diseases.

Just as no one is "cured" of diabetes, heart disease or an allergy to bee stings, once they have become addicted, no one

can be cured of an alcohol or other drug addiction. Nothing—
no magic pill, potion or hypnosis—has been developed that can
make an alcoholic drink like a normal person and stay that way
(in spite of endless attempts by researchers to do so).

But, like diabetes or heart disease, chemical dependency
can be arrested, and the victims can be treated so that they
recover from the symptoms and will stay that way through a
maintenance program.

Recovery from an addiction is not as elusive as it seems.
Millions of people can attest to that. And although each one
pursued it in a way most appropriate for them, there are some
common elements: abstinence, a program of recovery and a
spiritual foundation or strength.

Abstinence

The first step is to arrest the disease—to halt the progression. This is done through abstinence. It is just as absurd for a
recovering alcoholic to attempt maintenance drinking as it
would be for a person recovering from a poisoning to consider
"maintenance cyanide." Recovery from an ultimately fatal addiction demands total abstinence from the toxic chemical!

Considering the long-term mental, emotional and physical
effects and the awesome power of addiction, there is no conceiv-
able rationale for encouraging the addict's hopeless attempts
at "controlled use." Therefore, the basis of all recovery, the first
essential ingredient, is total abstinence.

Program of Living

Once the disease is arrested, it must be treated. The dependent cannot imagine surviving without the chemical, cannot cope with problems without the chemical and sees life as
totally unmanageable without the chemical.

When something is removed from a person's life, especially
the thing that dominated it, something else must fill the void
or else the person will relapse, switch addictions, commit
suicide or become a "dry drunk." The dry drunk is someone
who is not drinking but whose mental and emotional state have
not recovered. He displays the irrational behavior, blame, mood

swings, egotism, resentments, self-deception and uncontrolled anger of a drunk.

Thus something else is needed in recovery: to replace the chemical with an alternative means of surviving, coping and managing.

The recovering person must unlearn the destructive thinking and acting, and replace it with new attitudes and behaviors. This is called "a program of living."

A new way of life is the only option. It requires rigorous honesty, effective stress management, responsible actions and service to others. It breeds serenity, courage and wisdom. These are the basis for most successful recovery programs.

Through a new way of living, the dependent learns to tolerate and accept other people and past events as they are, address character defects, take care of business, make amends, talk openly about problems, seek the help of others and reach out to those in need. It is based on the principle that by helping others like you, you can better help yourself.

Attitude changes behavior. A program of living changes a person from the inside out, creating a brick-and-mortar foundation of self-esteem that can weather the maelstrom of personal crises.

One recovering person put it in easy terms: "I go to the gym every day to keep my muscle tone. If I don't, I lose it. I work my program of recovery daily to keep my mental tone, or I'll most certainly lose it."

A Spiritual Foundation

Carl Jung, the great psychotherapist, told an alcoholic patient, who had several relapses, that he could not help the man and that the medical and psychiatric professions had been unable to keep such alcoholics sober. He advised him that his only hope for recovery was a profound change of the spirit.

In a curious turn of events, Jung's former patient sought out the Oxford Group (a spiritually based mutual support fellowship). He recovered and helped someone else recover who inspired Bill W. (the founder of AA) to seek the spiritual experience that started his recovery and that of untold millions.

Whatever belief you may have in a Power greater than

yourself, the recovering person who calls on God, however perceived, finds a limitless supply of help—an Ultimate Authority who can prevail, no matter how deep the pit of addiction.

Through meditation and prayer, the dependent repairs the damage to his spirit, grows, commits to something beyond the travails of this lifetime and discovers an inexplicable mercy that quiets the craving and instills an abiding, inner peace.

Is That All There Is?

So sobriety, a program of living and spiritual growth are the basic ingredients of recovery. Survival was the best that early recovering addicts could hope for: to be sick and tired of being sick and tired, to trudge the road of happy destiny, and to strive to survive.

It once took 25 or 30 years of abuse before an addiction ran riot—when only alcohol was involved. Those who recovered usually did so in the twilight years of their lives. Today, things are different. Most dependents are addicted to alcohol in combination with psychoactive drugs, many of which are so potent that addiction happens quickly, sometimes with the first use. As in the case of so-called "designer drugs," which are specifically manufactured for their extreme potency, the synergism that speeds up and heightens the drugs' effect also speeds up the body's adaptation and demand for more.

When young people abuse such drugs, their dynamically growing bodies accelerate the response even further. They become addicted in a fraction of the time of an adult body. It is not unusual to find eight-year-old addicts. Unborn babies, sharing their addicted mothers' blood, are instantly addicted. One out of every 10 babies in this country is born chemically dependent.

Today more and more people "hit bottom" at 20 or 30. They enter recovery with the majority of their lifetime still ahead of them.

Younger people demand something much more powerful than the "hope of survival" to undergo the exhausting and terrifying labor of recovery. Somewhere there needs to be a shining reward inside the black hole of withdrawal. That something is achieving their fullest potential. It was the very search for such fulfillment that first misled the addict into the pit of pitiful, incomprehensible demoralization:

EPITAPH

I drank for happiness and became unhappy.
I drank for sociability and became lonely.
I drank for sophistication and became crude.
I drank for friendship and made enemies.
I drank to ease sorrow and sank in self-pity.
I drank for sleep and awakened weary.
I drank medicinally and became sick.
I drank for my job and lost my job.
I drank for relaxation and got the shakes.
I drank for courage and became afraid.
I drank to stimulate thought and blacked out.
I drank for conversation and forgot what I said.
I drank to feel heavenly and found hell.
I drank for power and became powerless.
I drank to erase problems and they multiplied.
I drank to cope with life and died.

—Anonymous

Full-Performance Recovery

Wanting fulfillment is not wrong—it is essential to survival. The addict found herself trapped when she sought that fulfillment through a chemical.

The objective of recovery is to help recovering people to reach their fullest human potential, to be all they can be straight and sober!

It goes beyond *survival* to *thrival*. It is simply called full-performance recovery.

To be fully self-actualizing, full-performance recovery involves goals, achievement, open communications and full performance, taking risks and building on the outcomes, using the life that God gave back to each recovering person and living it to its fullest, with sensitivity, humor and gratitude.

It is not enough to say, "I won't drink or drug no matter what." This is dryness or cleanness, not sobriety. It is unrealistic and irresponsible for a dry or clean addict to expect life to fall into place without playing an active role in that life.

The recovery adage "Let go and let God" has to do with outcomes, not responsibilities. God doesn't fill gas tanks.

The willpower of the recovering addict is restored—not to be able to drink or use again and control the drinking or using, that's impossible—but rather to take control of his or her own destiny, to make choices, to use to the fullest the talents and abilities restored in sobriety.

Full-performance recovery demands new skills to develop mentally, physically, emotionally, professionally, and spiritually. It includes learning how to open communication barriers so the addict can talk to his or her spouse and kids. It means exploring one's own spirituality and taking the steps to grow. It demands knowing how to solve problems, turn negatives into positives and cope positively with stress.

Fully recovered people take life as it comes, accept tragedy or loss and go on, reach out to others, let others in, demand honesty and integrity in all relationships, and they love unconditionally.

From Desperation to Inspiration

What happens to change a resistant, defiant and often belligerent dependent into someone willing to accept help? To find the answer, we can again look to the experience of those in self-help groups. Most "first timers" are against stopping and are as suspicious as thieves of any help—at first. They start attending meetings for the wrong reasons to "control" the drinking or because the judge ordered it, because the wife threatened to leave or because the boss said, "Do something."

But, after a few meetings, they gain enough sobriety to look around. They see people laughing and crying, working out their problems, enjoying a new-found freedom. Most stick around to find out their secret.

Desperation gets them to come. Inspiration keeps them coming back. They come for the wrong reasons and stay for the right ones.

AA members joke about the black heel marks on the sidewalks outside the meetings from being dragged in by their families and friends or by their own desperation—kicking, screaming and protesting.

They say that the real reason they started their own path to sobriety was simply to "get the heat off." They came at first to learn how to control their drinking, then later realized the only way to control it is to stop.

Joys of Recovery

To see a person rise from the cesspool of crack, smack or Jack Daniel's and soar to a life of ability, integrity and involvement is as thrilling as watching a child enter the world, vigorously suck in its first breath, squint at the light of its first day, reach out to the air and gustily yell out, "I'm here!"

It sounds unbelievable, but recovered addicts are grateful for the rocky road that led them to recovery and forced them to change the way they live. Today they are exciting, involved, concerned, committed. They operate without the seesaw morality and hidden agendas of "normal" people. They value their faith, family, friendships, performance, community and personal growth above all else.

They live their lives in fullest accountability, for anything less would mean relapse.

As one recovering person once said, "The butterfly is ever more blessed than the bird. Though both grace the heavens in the ecstasy of flight, the butterfly has known the drudgery of the crawl and the lonely confinement of the cocoon. His newfound freedom is richer, wilder, more thrilling than life itself."

This is recovery.

7

What Help Is Available?

◆

Larry stood on the street corner wildly waving his arms in the air. When a cop pulled over and asked him what he was doing, Larry blinked incredulously at the cop and said, "Keeping the asteroids away, of course!" The cop said, "There are no asteroids around here," and Larry nodded and continued his waving, "See! It works!"

Just as no two feet are alike, there is no one, guaranteed recovery program and no single approach that has worked for all recovered alcoholics and drug addicts. However, some programs have proven far more successful than others. A variety of resources exists for those who need help. You will want to examine the services available and learn something about how each works to be able to arrange the best possible course of action.

Treatment Programs

Patient care has come a long way since the days when alcoholics were condemned to live out the rest of their lives in insane asylums. In the 1920's the majority of the people in asylums treated regularly with sedatives were only alcoholic (displaying the temporary psychosis of a chemical dependency). As some alcoholics tell it: many died in captivity.

Today people with dependencies can choose from a wide array of treatment models that focus on the real problem—the addiction to a chemical.

Quality treatment programs offer the person with the disease and the family an outstanding opportunity for a full recovery, if sought in time.

These programs, which include in-patient and out-patient therapy, involve a period of intensive clinical care, usually between one and four weeks, after which the patient returns to active society while continuing to receive help on an out-patient or aftercare basis. There are three common treatment center models: the medically based counseling model, the psychiatric care model and the behavioral model. You should know something about each.

Over 7,000 treatment centers in the United States treat over two million people annually.

MEDICALLY BASED COUNSELING MODEL

Many of these are variations of a medically based counseling model which developed from programs at the Johnson Institute, St. Mary's and Hazelden in Minnesota.

This model emphasizes treating the mental, physical and spiritual aspects of the addiction in a whole-person approach. Physicians treat the body, counselors treat the mind and a spiritual director (usually a priest, rabbi or other minister) and the patient, through a personal program of prayer and meditation, address the spirit.

Mind, body and spirit are approached in three phases of treatment:

Phase I focuses primarily on the physical aspects of the disease, with detoxification, physical assessments, nutrition, and medication if prescribed.

Phase II focuses on the mental and emotional aspects of the disease and the recovery, with psychological assessments, a treatment plan, group and individual counseling for the patient and the family, both during and after treatment.

Phase III focuses on the spiritual aspects of recovery, with prayer and meditation, attending 12-step meetings and working the first steps of a 12-step spiritual program of recovery.

Also called "medical model" centers, these programs address alcohol and drug addiction as a disease. Available throughout the country, they may be free-standing, such as Hazelden or the Betty Ford Center, or established as wings of existing health care facilities, such as the treatment units of hospitals and medical centers. They may also be state or locally operated indigent care centers.

Patients reside in semi-private rooms on the premises and undergo 24-hour medical care following a period of detoxification. The program includes medical assessments, treatment for any damage the disease has done physically, individual and group counseling sessions, nutritional care and usually the availability of a 12-step self-help group. Some centers offer separate programs for men and women, or for "impaired health professionals."

Nearly 30% of the patients in counseling model treatment centers admitted themselves without an intervention. Some appeared on the doorstep and checked themselves in. Others called in advance for a tour and admitted themselves at a later date.

Where an intervention is needed, an interventionist connected with the center will review the person's dependency condition with you, help the family arrange financial details and conduct the intervention.

Most counseling model centers include staff members who are recovering, thereby fostering a mutual compassion and self-help support between patients and recovering staff. The emotionally bankrupt addict is "loved" to wellness by others who have shared some of the same experiences, understand and are successfully recovering from the same addiction.

Each center will vary in the emphasis placed on nutrition, physical fitness, spiritual growth, family program and participation in local 12-step group. Some will include relaxed, noninstitutionalized living, outdoor experiences or weekend outings to help patients develop positive ways to relax and have fun. If freedom of movement is desired, free-standing facilities are available. Because of the nature of a general hospital or similar health care facility and its responsibility to other crisis patients, freedom of movement may be somewhat restricted, although recreation periods and outings are often included.

The strongest centers address addiction as a family disease by offering family treatment care and aftercare programs. The most successful programs include in the cost of treatment at least a year of weekly aftercare group meetings with a professional counselor to address the day-to-day problems of recovery.

To summarize, the elements of a good medically based counseling model program are:

1. Medical and psychiatric assessments.
2. Individualized treatment plans.
3. Individual and group counseling.
4. Self-help group support.
5. Ongoing program of living.
6. Family program.
7. Nutrition and fitness.
8. Living skills.
9. Aftercare (weekly group counseling for one to two years).
10. 24-hour nursing care.

No one treatment program is all things to all people. Counseling model centers embody many of the most successful approaches known today, and at least seven out of every ten patients begin their recovery immediately. However, chemical dependency is so onerous that as many as one out of three patients relapses before recovering—experimenting to make sure that they really cannot control the addiction. Most do return to 12-step meetings or treatment and find lasting recovery.

PSYCHIATRIC MODEL

Some treatment programs follow a psychiatric model which focuses on treating the mind of the chemically dependent person.

Psychiatric centers can be found as independent clinics, institutions or as wings of state hospitals or mental health institutions. They usually employ a staff psychiatrist, psychologists and medical personnel. In- and out-patient programs are available. Treatment is dramatically individualized, especially in the larger institutions where multiple disorders are treated and where patients differ greatly in the nature and severity of their illnesses.

The philosophy of psychiatric care centers varies widely. Many do not recognize the disease concept of addiction, but classify it as a mental illness. Some routinely treat addiction through psychoanalysis. There is disagreement on the effectiveness of this approach for primary alcohol and drug addiction. Because of the action of mind-altering chemicals on the brain to create denial, all addicts blame other people—and a past that cannot be changed—for their problems. Focusing on the patient's perception of the past as the cause of the present can prolong the period before the addict accepts the reality of his addiction, achieves total abstinence, takes responsibility for his own actions and begins working a program of recovery.

Psychiatric attention is vital in those cases where the dependent is also suffering from a chronic psychosis, as in the case of manic depressives, schizophrenics, psychotics, psychopaths and sociopaths.

Depending on the testing mechanism, between 5% and 10% of alcoholics are found to suffer from "secondary addiction." In other words, their primary problem is not a chemical dependency but a chronic psychosis.

Such people need both a program of recovery and some form of continuing psychiatric attention (usually including a prescription medication to control the psychosis). Without it, attempts at sobriety will repeatedly fail.

For this reason, many treatment centers offer a counseling model with psychiatric services available. Dual-diagnostic centers (centers that offer both addiction treatment and psychiatric care) specialize in diagnosing and treating both primary and secondary addictions. In most cases, the psychiatric problem can be addressed in a longer therapy program, and many psychiatric patients may eventually be able to lead a life of recovery without the prescription medication.

If in doubt, a professional interventionist can arrange for a psychological assessment and diagnosis.

Psychiatric care can also be a beneficial complement to counseling model treatment centers when the dependency involves sexual abuse issues. It can also complement aftercare when the primary objective is to prevent the responses that will trigger a relapse and when it is part of a larger program which focuses on abstinence, a program of living and participation in a 12-step recovery group.

BEHAVIORAL MODEL/AVERSION THERAPY

The behavioral school of psychology emphasizes the role of conditioning in the treatment of addiction—again focusing attention on the mental aspect of the disease. Some centers rely on negative reinforcement to create a deep psychological "aversion" to using the addictive chemical.

Called "aversion therapy centers," they use ills, pills or chills to shake the dependent out of the addiction.

Some administer large quantities of alcohol, making patients physically ill and placing them in a room with mirrors so they can witness their violent physical and mental responses. Some employ shock therapy—electrical shocks sent whenever the person picks up a drink or drug. Some rely primarily on administering averse drugs, like Antabuse, which cause the addict to become violently ill if alcohol is taken while the averse drug remains in the patient's system.

Many such centers have been criticized for being "revolving door" institutions where patients have had to return several times before achieving any period of abstinence.

For most addicts, once the negative stimulus is no longer present, the compulsion to use eventually overrides the brain's remembered aversion. Most aversion therapy programs require repeated follow-up treatments. Just as the jail is no deterrent to a chronic drunk driver, pain and violent illness are no deterrent to an addict who daily endures physical and emotional pain rather than give up his chemical.

Chronic relapse for patients in aversion therapy is most often blamed on programs where patients have not regained self-esteem, their lives have not changed, their attitudes and ability to solve problems have not improved, and they lack a significant base of support. Many such programs have been modified to include 12-step programs and group support.

Selecting a Treatment Program

In selecting a treatment program, check first to make sure that the program is licensed, the counselors are certified alcohol and drug counselors and, if possible, the program is accredited by the Joint Commission on Accreditation of Health Care Institutions, Inc., or another nationally recognized group which maintains standards for diagnosis, care, hygiene, safety, record keeping, and follow-up. Unfortunately, most accrediting processes have no way of evaluating program quality and long-term program effectiveness, so the best evaluation is usually in talking with former patients and their family members and friends. Also check the terms and conditions of your available insurance coverage, as this may determine the kind of program you select. If insurance coverage is not available, you may be able to work out a payment plan, an arrangement with an employer or state assistance. Some centers have access to financial aid for those with limited income.

Mutual Aid Support Groups

Mutual aid support groups offer an immediate, hands-on therapy by and for people who share the same chemical problem.

The quintessential model of successful mutual aid is the 12-step approach of Alcoholics Anonymous. Founded in 1935, the program and its virtually limitless 12-step imitators (Narcotics Anonymous, Al-Anon, as well as groups for cocaine addicts, overeaters, sexual addicts, emotional addicts, smokers, gamblers and adult children of addicts) is responsible for the vast majority of recovering people throughout the world. There are over 85,270 AA groups alone in 34 countries worldwide.

Until AA, attempts to treat alcoholism had been largely unsuccessful or limited in scope. Then, as reported in the second edition of *Alcoholics Anonymous:* "Of alcoholics who came to AA and really tried, 50% got sober at once and remained that way, 25% sobered up after some relapses, and the remainder of those who stayed on with AA showed improvement." Although no empirical data exist, recent AA membership surveys support the same findings. The program's effectiveness for long-term recovery has led most treatment programs to include it as an essential ingredient in their treatment plans.

Members of AA represent men and women of every age, faith and ethnic origin. Millionaires and dropouts, astronauts and miners, former White House residents and indigents have found recovery through AA's 12 steps.

Originally composed mostly of people who suffered from alcoholism alone, AA today is largely people recovering from dual or multiple addictions which include alcohol. AA's usually call themselves recovered or "recovering" alcoholics, always mindful that they can never be cured of the effect alcohol has on them if they drink. They have, however, recovered from their compulsion to drink, their dependency on alcohol to cope and their dysfunctional behavior.

It is suggested that members attend meetings, abstain from alcohol between meetings, work the 12 steps and choose a sponsor to help them. The 12 steps include admitting hopelessness, asking God for help as each understands God, becoming honest with oneself, making amends to others and helping others who suffer from the same disease. How each person applies the AA program is a matter of personal choice, as is that person's view of a Higher Power (which, for the faithless, morally destitute alcoholic, may be nothing more than the table around which people like him have recovered).

Those who attend AA maintain the anonymity of all whom they meet there. "Who you see here, what they say here, when you leave here, let it stay here."

AA charges no dues or membership fees and has no requirements other than the "desire" to stop drinking—even if a person has not yet been able to stop.

Most 12-step groups publish a phone number in the local directory and offer a full-time answering service. Someone on a "call list" will return your call and answer any questions.

"Open" meetings are open to family, friends, community and anyone to wants to learn more about the 12-step program.

The members of 12-step programs like to show others how it works. Meetings usually last 60 or 90 minutes and are scheduled at various locations throughout the week. "Closed" meetings are for those who admit they have a specific dependency.

You may want to attend an open meeting to learn more about the disease and the recovery. A good way to support another person's recovery is to attend Al-Anon, the self-help meetings specifically for families and friends of alcoholics. The 12 steps, which advocate honesty, gratitude, amends, service and prayer, are an excellent way for anyone to get more out of life. You'll not only help the person you care about, but you'll learn something for yourself as well!

Public and Community Resources

A wide range of community resources exists to help people address chemical dependencies, including federally supported national hot lines for alcohol and cocaine addiction, locally supported regional crisis hot lines and community action agencies and teams.

Detoxing should always be medically supervised. Detoxification facilities are available at local hospitals, although detoxing is not enough to stop a chemically dependent person's continued use. Very few dependents are able to voluntarily quit after detoxing without additional help.

Several hospitals, medical clinics and treatment centers offer full-time community outreach personnel trained in chemical dependency.

Many employers offer a full-time employee assistance officer to work with personnel who have alcohol and drug problems, arranging for the employees to get care and keep their jobs. In mid-sized firms, these responsibilities are handled by the personnel officer. Alcohol and drug treatment is covered under many employee benefits packages. In some cases employers will help cover the cost of getting help; they have found it is far more costly to hire and train a new employee than to rehabilitate the current one.

Many communities have full-time chemical dependency police officers, social workers and education counselors to address problems affecting children, shelter and employment. Most local alcohol and drug task forces keep a listing of available resources. Contact your local government, health department or chamber of commerce for more information.

Alcohol/Drug Counselors

Alcohol and drug counselors are professional counselors and psychologists who specialize in treating chemical dependencies.

They work with patients and their families on an in- or outpatient basis, can arrange for treatment if it is necessary and can guide the dependent through the steps of a recovery program.

Check in your phone directory under "Counselors: Alcohol and Drug." Call and ask questions. You may find a great variety of philosophies and approaches ranging from those who counsel for a particular dependency to those who treat dependency with hypnosis or acupuncture.

Look for the initials C.A.C. (certified alcohol counselor), C.D.C. (certified drug counselor), C.A.D.C. (certified alcohol and drug counselor), or C.E.A.P. (certified employee assistance professional).

Check the counselor's credentials and licensing in alcohol and drug therapy. If possible, let others know you are looking and seek referrals. (This may be difficult due to the confidentiality issue.) Select someone who has worked with and is recommended by an accredited dependency treatment center.

Private Therapists/Mental Health Clinics

These are professionals who hold doctorates or master's degrees in social work or psychology. They can provide excellent services for bringing chemically dependent families back together and for helping people address problems in their lives.

However, analysts, psychologists and social workers without extensive experience in alcohol and drug dependency may fail to see the behavior and thinking which is purely chemically related and may treat the symptom instead of the cause.

Addicts are usually adept at hiding their dependency from

their families, physicians and therapists, using the attention to emotional disorders or stress as a sheepskin to get the "heat off" from family and employers while continuing to drink or use, as well as to obtain prescription sedatives and painkillers.

Several independent counseling services are available and advertised in your local phone book. You would be wise to check around. If possible, speak with former clients. Unless there are other disorders involved, it is best to find an addictions specialist recommended by your local treatment center.

Chaplains

Priests, rabbis and ministers are professionals well trained and gifted in addressing human problems and spiritual needs. They vary greatly, however, in their training, understanding of and exposure to chemical dependency.

Some are recovering themselves and regularly share their experience, strength and hope with others in the recovering community, while some consider dependency to be a moral weakness, sinful defiance or willful disobedience, and reject the disease concept.

Chaplains can guide and encourage the addict to turn his life over to the care of God, maintain personal honesty, take a moral inventory, make amends and share with others who suffer from the same dependency—all essential to the recovery process. They can help addicts overcome barriers to spiritual growth and discover deeper prayer and meditation.

Miracles do happen. Many people (including members of AA) have had conversion experiences in which their craving was removed entirely in prayer. And these addicts have found it essential to make major changes in their lives, be responsible and be ever-mindful that they can never be "cured" of chemical dependency to the point where they can drink or use again without far worse relapse.

Choose the help of a chaplain experienced in chemical dependency who understands the disease concept. If possible, select the help of someone who supports 12-step recovery groups.

Essential Criteria for Effective Help

Whatever resources you choose, remember that the dependent will have the best chance of recovery if they include the following elements:

1. Persons trained in treating chemical dependencies
2. Required abstinence from mood-altering chemicals
3. A program of responsible living
4. A support group of recovering addicts
5. A spiritual base

CONDUCTING AN INTERVENTION

◆

"Giles. You've got to get a grip on your life. You're 35 and you haven't got a lot of it left! If you keep up with the cocaine, you're gonna die."

"I hate to tell ya this, Dee. We're all gonna die."

"Yea, but the idea is to do it at the end of life. Not in the middle."

"Why?"

"Uh, because. . . . Well. Uh. . . . You owe it to your mother. Have you ever given birth?"

◆

Preparing for an intervention means knowing whom to involve, what to say and when to say it to have the greatest impact.

How to Prepare: Who, What, When and Where?

◆

"If the only thing we have to fear is fear itself, HELP!!!"

All right. You agree that there needs to be a concerned-other intervention as soon as possible. But WHO should do it? You or *another* other?

First, never intervene alone. The more intervenors, the harder it is for the dependent to deny, lie or manipulate. Moreover, the more people present, the less likely he will be to act irrationally or to try to intimidate the intervenor.

Second, only involve those people who (1) know firsthand about the person's abuse or the addictive behavior and agree there is a serious problem, (2) care about the abuser and are able to convey their message in a nonjudgmental, nonpunitive and loving way, and (3) are prepared to intervene (informed, alert, directed). Only they will be able to deliver the critical message of tough love convincingly.

By taking the initiative to read this far, you have shown that you are personally aware of the problem, you care about the dependent, you are willing to spend the time necessary to learn about the dependency and the alternatives and you are willing to be involved in some way. You have met the basic qualifications for a good intervenor.

You'll be an essential ingredient on the team whether or not you lead the intervention.

But your head is probably full of questions and your heart is certainly full of dread. That's encouraging. You'd have to be crazy or comatose not to feel a little anxiety at the idea of attacking the dragon Dependency unprotected and unarmed. This chapter will address the first part, protection.

To put it bluntly, the dependent will honestly think that the intervenor is threatening his life! He cannot imagine surviving without the drug. His only hope is to disarm his "oppressor."

Since his only defense is offense, he'll try to use it. Most likely it will be an assault targeted at the intervenor's motives and fears. To intervene, you must disengage from your reactions, learn to step back and put your emotions on hold.

What Are Your Motives or Motivations?

This is a good time to examine your motives or motivations. The dependent will challenge them, so whatever they are, you'll need to be open and honest about them!

Don't judge them good or bad. For the moment, they simply ARE. So, identify and address them.

Love: You love the dependent. Maybe you no longer have a reason to, but you do. You'll do whatever is necessary to free her of the bondage.

Survival: The addict's behavior is threatening your life or your job. If you don't do something now, you'll lose in some way your home, family, savings, reputation, performance record, clients, accounts, credibility, friends, whatever.

Altruism: You want to help save a life and the lives of all the others who are affected. You care about the well-being of others.

Social Responsibility: Addiction turns good people into sick people who hurt themselves and others. Everyone pays in ever-increasing ways. If someone doesn't step forward soon, the price tag will exceed what any of us can afford.

Sanity: The addict is driving you crazy and making your life hell. It's time to do something.

Deflection: While focusing on others' problems, you avoid attention to the serious problems in your own life.

Duty: You're doing this because you've been advised to by your boss, physician, psychotherapist, clients, family, etc. It's your duty.

Annoyance: You are a responsible person. It annoys you when someone else isn't. (Watch out! Perfectionism is the only socially acceptable form of suicide. It keeps others from getting close to you and keeps you from fully appreciating yourself.)

Personal Gain: You stand to gain financially or otherwise by exposing the dependent's problem or removing him from the scene: to gain a job, promotion, reward, custody of children, property, business or relationship with another. If such is the case, first consult a professional about your involvement in the intervention. If you can't be honest, it's best for all if you stay out of the intervention and get help for yourself.

Revenge: You are angry at the dependent and want to see him pay his dues. If anger is your motive, talk with a counselor. Your anger will sabotage the intervention.

Fears and Resistance

Similarly, you may have just as many feelings pulling you away from the intervention as pushing you into it. If you understand them, it will make it easier for you to deal with them positively.

Change: No one likes imposed change. For whatever reason, it threatens security. By forcing the dependent to change, you cause major changes in your life. Things were tough, but predictable. Now the future is an "unknown."

Losing Your Role: You may like your role as martyr, hero or major general. Such roles are called "enablers," because they rely on the addict's weakness, hide the dependency from outsiders and postpone the addict's accountability. Once healthy and able to take responsibility for himself, the dependent won't need a nursemaid, mother-figure or guardian. Your role will change. You'll lose some responsibility and power. You may never again be "needed," used or manipulated. You will be respected and loved.

Rejection: Others may misjudge your motives or resent you for interfering. They believe it is better to die of dependency if one must, as long it's done discreetly. Or you may be afraid of losing the dependent's love. By exposing the addiction, you will permanently damage a long-term love relationship—the one between the abuser and the drug! He'll resent you every day until he recovers. Then he'll think you walk on water.

Inadequacy: You may feel that the person's dependency is a result of your shortcomings, or that calling for others to help is a public admission that you cannot handle the problem yourself. Such feelings are natural but groundless. You did not create the biology or psychosis of dependency. You cannot change other people, no matter how much you love them. With education, however, you can change your responses and often cause others to change themselves. There is no place for guilt in a chemical dependency. Blame the chemical. What is past is past. The future begins now.

Failure: You may be afraid of doing the wrong thing, thereby causing the intervention to fail. Remember, you are battling an insidious disease. Often the disease wins. It will most assuredly win if you don't try to stop it. If this intervention doesn't work, it has, at least, ended the denial.

Chemical Dependency: Because of heredity and social factors, it is not unusual to find early or mid-stage dependency among some of the dependent's close family and friends. It could be that your own use has progressed beyond "seeking a swing." Blowing the whistle may attract attention. Be honest. If you suspect you have a problem, get help.

Retaliation: You've seen this person angry and you're afraid of retaliation. Nothing diffuses a threat-maker more than confronting him in an atmosphere of care and concern—which is what an intervention does. Your show of strength says, simply, you're not going to take it anymore. (Note: If the person has physically injured you or others before or is likely to do so, remove yourself from danger and notify the proper agencies. Do not attempt to intervene without first seeking professional help.) Most addicts eat, work and sleep with the fear of being locked up, away from their drug. Usually, the threat from a judge, attorney, social services person or other third party offers an effective deterrent. Always protect yourself.

Understanding Co-dependency

Anyone whose life is altered because of the actions of a chemically dependent person is co-dependent. A co-dependent can be a family member, friend, boss or co-worker. (See Appendix D.)

Someone once said, "A co-dependent is a centipede waiting for the other shoe to drop." No matter how many shoes drop or what comes down, there's always more up there. Things always get worse.

Regrettably, close relatives will often wait too long before spearheading an intervention, trying to postpone consequences that will reflect on the family by "coping." Yet they are the ones who should be the first to yell HALT! The abuse affects them directly. It causes dysfunctional families with dysfunctional kids who grow up, marry and have dysfunctional families, and on and on.

Statistics show that family members are more likely to suffer injury or death as a result of the addiction than the addict. For your sake, it's best to stop it early.

Addiction is considered infectious because it poisons everyone close to the addict, even though the co-dependent family members or friends may not even drink or use. They suffer from the disease because they have learned to lie, manipulate, carry resentments, blame, martyr-play, hero-play and hide their true feelings from everyone else.

They are so used to walking on robin's eggs and carrying a big feather that the idea of confronting the problem head-on terrifies them.

The co-dependent family lives an illusion it creates to maintain the appearance of family stability for the outside world. But soon the distortion, cover-ups, excuses and alibis destroy the family on the inside.

Many families resist help, thinking that by drawing attention to the problem, they are acknowledging their collective failure. They feel guilty that the dependent ever needed a chemical to cope or escape in the first place.

Spouses are naturally afraid of losing something familiar (someone with whom they've learned to survive) in favor of a great unknown:

"Maybe Marty won't love me when his brain clears."

"Sue's okay. All she needs is a double martini and a back rub when she gets home."

"When Brad gets clean we may discover that we never knew each other and really don't even like each other!"

Because of their fears, family and friends will try to cover up the problem, minimize it or affix blame elsewhere (most often on themselves). They enable.

(Some recovering wives joke about the way they enabled. They say they had the "Queen Isabella Syndrome" with their addicted husbands. Columbus, after all, wasn't sure where he was going. He didn't know where he was once he got there. When he returned, he didn't know where he'd been. And the whole thing was financed by a woman!)

Because it is a family disease, chemical dependency demands a family recovery.

Family members need to seek out a program to heal and grow together, whether in a 12-step environment (Al-Anon, Nar-Anon, Alateen, Families Anonymous or Adult Children of Alcoholics), family treatment or family counseling. Otherwise the old behaviors begin again, and, consequently, so does the pattern for continued chemical dependency.

Returning a healthy person to a sick environment is like curing a man of black-lung disease and then sending him back into the mine that gave it to him! It can only result in further sickness and a more devastating relapse.

Recovery demands that everyone affected—the dependent, the family and close friends—admit the problem and confront it, and then seek out the services necessary to heal themselves.

Who Should Be on the Team?

A group of as little as two may work for some interventions, especially in the workplace. As many as ten can be very effective for a community intervention, thus confronting the dependent with the full impact of his or her actions.

Remember the qualifications. Intervenors should: (1) know firsthand of the abuse or the problems resulting from the addictive behavior, (2) care about the welfare of the dependent, and (3) prepare themselves.

Here is a checklist of possible team members for the intervention. A group of three to five is best.

- Spouse
- Parents
- Children
- Brother/sister
- Close friends (or former friends)
- Co-workers
- Business associates
- Boss/supervisor (or former boss)
- Client
- Personal physician
- Extended family (uncle, in-laws, etc.)
- Minister
- Estranged spouse
- Recovered friend or acquaintance
- Counselor or interventionist (if needed)

Recruiting and preparing the team is a lot easier than it sounds, and works well for a spontaneous as well as a planned intervention.

Call the people with the most firsthand experience and influence on the dependent (closest family, friends, business associates, etc.). Explain the problem and the progression of the disease. Ask if they are willing to give a couple of hours of their time to help out or at least to find out more.

The Planning Session

Schedule a time when everyone who has agreed to help can get together for an informal planning session at a location unknown to the dependent. It is best to allow at least two hours for the preparation.

Welcome the participants and, if necessary, introduce them

to each other. Since everyone present has volunteered their time, energy and concern, thank them and share the hope that the problem you have in common (as "concerned others") will soon be resolved. Briefly summarize the situation with the dependent and why an intervention is needed now.

Explain that the purpose of the planning session is to learn what an intervention is, how it works and what each person can do to assure that it will be a success. It is also an opportunity to compare experiences, share some feelings and support each other.

Ask that everything said in the room and in the intervention be held in confidence among those present.

Describe what usually happens in an intervention. You may want to refer to the definition for concerned-other intervention (page 64).

Review the purposes of an intervention:

- To communicate everyone's care and concern.
- To give everyone an opportunity to confront the dependent with the facts of his/her behavior, thereby presenting inarguable evidence.
- To convince the dependent to seek a specific type of help (or an option of two choices) by giving ultimatums that the group will enforce.
- If possible, to immediately enroll the person in a recovery program by making advance arrangements and having someone present to escort her.

In short, the intervention is creating "the bottom" for the addict. It's a place where each person has a chance to make the biggest impression. Some people may not be sure about whether to participate. Emphasize that participation is completely voluntary, but that together it is possible to do what cannot be done individually. With each person playing a small role, the impossible becomes manageable.

The planning session should then give participants the information they need to intervene. Here are some helpful tasks and tools to include in the planning session.

A brief overview of what addiction is and some of its signs.

You may wish to begin by reading aloud to the group "Understanding the Dependent" (page 101) and then reviewing the "Stages of Dependency" chart (pages 30–31).

Identifying the important facts concerning the dependent's behavior. Each participant should be encouraged to remember the most recent problem, what occurred and how it made them respond and feel. They should do the same for the previous incident and as far back as they can remember. One useful tool is the form entitled, "Listing the Objective Facts" (Appendix C). Each person should make up his own record. It will shed light on the incidents that have made an intervention necessary, give everyone a chance to compare experiences and become vital information for the intervention.

Identifying the participants' personal feelings about the dependent and the dependency. It is important to discuss and release unpleasant feelings (such as anger, resentment and frustration) in a constructive way before the intervention. Discussing pleasant, supportive feelings (such as compassion, hope and love) will help enhance the intervention. A helpful tool is the "Emotions and Feelings Checklist" (Appendix B).

Reviewing how an intervention works. The four steps of an intervention from Chapter 9 should be discussed so that the group can identify opportunities during the intervention for each person to share facts and feelings.

Selecting a chairperson. A person should be selected to lead the intervention who is emotionally detached from the dependent, usually someone other than the spouse, parent or child. This person's role is to guide the intervention, give everyone a chance to speak, convey love and concern and remain calm.

Selecting the Recovery Ultimatum(s). Participants should choose the ultimatums that will motivate the person into a specific recovery program, and who will communicate and carry them out. (See Chapter 13.)

Deciding when and where the intervention will take place, who will chair and the order in which each person will speak.

Deciding who will contact the dependent and how he will arrive at the place of the intervention. This can be done by arranging a fictitious meeting or social affair or by surprising the dependent at a particular stop during his daily routine.

The participants should arrange to meet at the location a

half-hour before the dependent is scheduled to arrive to re-hearse the four steps and what each person will say.

The approach we offer here is a suggested guideline. Modify it to fit your needs and those of the group. Sometimes excellent opportunities create themselves. For example, four sons took turns intervening alone on their dad during a reunion weekend, leading up to the final confrontation on the morning of their departure when dad's luggage appeared in the hallway next to their own. One family intervened on their son at his birthday when the box he opened contained all his paraphernalia and copies of school and police records. Three businessmen inter-vened on an associate in the back of a commuter plane. A coach and his team intervened on a player in the locker room after losing a game. A group of friends intervened on their host during a pleasure cruise when they were 40 miles offshore. Some parishioners intervened on their pastor during a retreat weekend.

Finding Out More

For an added advantage, you may want to review Chapter 10, "Anticipating the Dependent's Response." Try to predict the dependent's response by identifying the dependent's preferred way of reacting (ActionStyle) and how best to respond to it. Pick a few main points to communicate to the addict. Focus on just those.

Those who want more background information should read Chapter 12: How to Respond to Typical Arguments, or obtain their own copy of this book. You'll find other resource books listed in the bibliography.

Some treatment centers offer community intervention classes that provide excellent preparation for those desiring more intensive training.

Remember that if you need some guidance or old-fashioned hand-holding, there are professionals and volunteer members of self-help groups who are ready and willing to help you.

When Is Best?

When do you hold the intervention? Addiction always worsens the longer it continues. The sooner the intervention, the better. Not doing anything is worse than not doing it well.

The best interventions are often spontaneous, whenever there's a crack in the door or right after a crisis caused by the alcohol or drug abuse—an arrest or accident. Sometimes the dependent will invite the intervention by commenting, "I'm having a little trouble with my temper lately," or "My memory isn't what it used to be." If the family or friends are prepared in advance, they can let the best opportunity present itself. When the opportunity arises, do it.

UNDERSTANDING THE DEPENDENT

(Everyone involved in the intervention should read this. It will help set the stage for a caring and effective confrontation.)

When you have been forced to live with, work with or otherwise depend on a person who is chronically mind-altered, you are dependent on chemical dependency.

You are probably angry, frustrated, scared, bewildered and disgusted by a person who is doing something to you that you would never do to anyone else. Naturally, you can't understand why. Oftentimes, love is a questionable commodity.

The addict is not himself or herself, but someone "under the influence" of a mind-altering chemical who is powerless over the biology of his or her own body. The dependent can no more control the craving than you can control the urge to urinate.

Certainly, the dependent must be held responsible for his or her behavior even under the influence. That's both the law and the ticket to recovery. Called "reality therapy," a person must acknowledge responsibility and pay the price to be freed of the past and move forward, or else be bound to carry the past forever.

Law and order would go bonkers if the defense "not guilty by reason of insanity" applied unilaterally to a person under the influence of a drug. There would never be another arrest for driving out of control, assault, child abuse or murder when a chemical was involved. People must be held accountable.

But the intervention is not a place for punishment. It is a place for guided compassion. Justice will come in recovery when the person voluntarily finds ways to make up for the past.

Most often, an addict is not a bad person who needs to get better, but a sick person who needs to get well.

Don't wait for a "bottom" before doing anything, or the dependent will dig a hole clear through and out the other side of the planet.

A bottom can be anywhere a person wants it to be. People no longer have to lose their Reeboks and sleep under freeway overpasses before they are ready to accept help.

When intoxicated, the alcoholic may be more confident, agreeable and pliable and you may have an easier time—although he may not remember anything you said (and you want him to remember the intervention the rest of his life!). However, if a person is willing to accept help when intoxicated or medicated, and help is immediately available, don't wait! Usually the morning after, during a period of remorse, is an excellent time. But don't let time pass. Once he begins to crave again, he'll promise the world and then break his promise. For most drugs, once the effect wears off and withdrawal sets in, the addict's only concern is getting more—and it's not at a recovery center! That's when you'll need to be tougher, want more people to back you up and have the force of some Recovery Ultimatums behind you.

Whatever you decide, remember the old girl's "scout" motto: Be Prepared (because he never is)!

Proceed on the assumption than no time is a good one, and now may be the only time you'll ever have.

Where and How

Where you hold the intervention communicates nonverbally the freedoms and the restrictions on behavior. Therefore, never hold an intervention in the dependent's home. Seek neutral ground, such as the home or office of a friend, a community room or a church hall.

Rehearse the intervention in the room where it will occur. If possible, rehearse in the hour beforehand. Arrange the dependent's seat as far away from the door as possible. Participants' seats should face the dependent, and can be in a semicircle, as long as others are seated between him and the door. Arrange for the dependent to go to the location for a meeting or social event. Do not forewarn him about the intervention. It must be a surprise. Intervention by invitation doesn't work.

Everyone should be standing when the dependent enters the room, is welcomed and is shown to his seat. Then the intervention can begin.

What's the Recovery Objective?

Decide the Recovery Objective of the intervention beforehand—the type of help most appropriate for the dependent. In- or out-patient treatment? Self-help group? Independent counseling? A community service? Is it available now, and if not, when? Check insurance coverage or financial aid. Make all arrangements in advance of the intervention.

If you leave these decisions to the dependent, don't be surprised to find that the intervention will end and nothing will happen. Given a chance, the dependent will always find something wrong with whatever help is suggested and will procrastinate until everyone else walks away. So, don't suggest. You choose, or give the dependent a choice between two options that you have arranged. It simply doesn't work any other way.

Calling in the Authorities

As the addiction progresses and the dependent keeps increasing the dosage to achieve the desired effect, he believes his body is tolerating the increase. But because each body is different, no one can predict when a toxic reaction will occur. If you encounter someone who has overdosed or displays bizarre physical or emotional behavior, call for medical attention immediately. Do not try to handle it yourself.

Sometimes a person will decide to quit cold turkey and

attempt to handle the withdrawal alone. A person should never try detoxing without supervision. Insist that the dependent enter a medical detox ward until withdrawal is complete.

At other times, the dependent will become violent and will threaten everyone who tries to come between him and his addiction.

When a dependency goes out of control, leaving everyone around feeling scared and helpless about what to do, or if the chemical dependency causes the person to become a threat to himself or others, do not hesitate to call for help, even if an intervention is scheduled.

Notifying the appropriate medical, social and legal personnel does three things: It gets the dependent's attention. It protects everyone involved. And it provides an objective documentation of the dependency problem—one which can prove invaluable in a later intervention. Here are some options:

Emergency Medical Technologists: If the dependent has accidentally or intentionally injured himself or another, or is overdosing, call for emergency help and get medical attention immediately—either through the local ambulance service or a 911 number, if available. This is important even if you think the situation might not turn out to be serious.

Police: Police are trained to handle drug-induced violent behavior and trauma. As many as 70% of police reports involve alcohol and drug related incidents, including assaults, rapes, misconduct, traffic and water accidents and driving under the influence, as well as drug possession and trafficking.

Social Services Agencies and Crisis Centers: Most cities and counties employ staff to work primarily with families of chemically dependent persons, providing food, housing and counseling assistance. Many have specialists to handle victim protection, crisis and care. All offer special offices to investigate reports of possible child abuse.

Community and Religious Outreach Groups: These will offer assistance and shelters to those in need—including a safe place for those who have been physically threatened and cannot return to their homes.

Treatment and Recovery Centers: These usually employ a full-time community services person who is available for emergencies. Most will also visit your home or workplace to assist you, provide treatment information and arrange an interview or intervention, if requested.

Hospitals and Walk-in Clinics: These will administer the immediate medical attention needed. A medical report is customary.

Family Physician: Family physicians usually treat the physical effects of chemical abuse—a persistent bruising or broken bones from fights or falls, respiratory or heart problems, anemia, seizures, etc. If forewarned, they can examine the patient for the physical signs of a chemical dependency.

Psychologist or Psychiatrist: If there is evidence that a person poses a legitimate threat to himself or others, a licensed psychologist or psychiatrist can prepare the documents to commit the person to a psychiatric examination, in most states.

Judge: Many states have made it easy for next-of-kin to obtain court orders to commit persons to treatment who have lost their ability to stop drinking or using drugs or otherwise pose a threat to themselves or others. Where alcohol or drugs are found in the blood of a defendant, a judge can sentence the person to attend a certain number of 12-step meetings or accept treatment. If a person has threatened others with physical harm, a court order can be obtained which prevents the individual, under penalty of jail, from contacting those he has threatened.

Wherever possible, obtain a copy of the admission, treatment, police, court or other report for each incident. By calling for outside help, you are doing the dependent person and family an invaluable service—bringing attention to a situation that will only worsen until someone is seriously hurt. You are also gathering powerful evidence of the dependency that will add fuel to the intervention.

If you are threatened, there are two rules to remember:

1. Notify the authorities.
2. Don't rely on them. Take whatever measures are necessary to protect yourself.

9

How an Intervention Works

◆

"I know you think you understood what I said, but what I said wasn't what I meant."

Communicating to Be Heard

We were all born with ears and a mouth, the ability to hear and to speak—an awesome capability. But no one gave us an operator's manual on how to be good listeners and effective communicators. Somehow the ears don't work so well when the mouth is open.

Maybe your sentences never run on and you've never been caught with your participle dangling, and maybe you can talk your way out of a speeding ticket on the Pennsylvania Turnpike with a fuzz buster on your dash. Maybe you know how to win friends and influence politicians. Fine. This is different.

What you are learning here is how to communicate effectively when the object of your intentions is drunk, angry or both, you have little time, and you aren't sure why the hell you even got involved in the first place.

Next to a kiss or a clobber, an intervention is probably the world's most effective form of communication. It's a constructive confrontation with an urgency or emergency message delivered with maximum care, respect and concern.

If carried out, the intervention will deliver the clearest message of the dependent's entire life: You have a disease, it's progressed, everyone cares about you, but no one is taking the abuse any longer. Here are the choices or else here is what we're going to do.

After an intervention, the dependent can no longer pawn off the dependency as anything else. There are no exits. The puzzle parts will never again fit together in the neat way that they did in denial.

If you typically avoid confrontations of any kind, intervening is no less intimidating than jumping naked into a cage with a snarling, salivating lion.

But what happens in a concerned-other intervention is usually a surprise. Most often, the wild beast will snort and snarl a little and then quickly turn into a quaking lamb who is willing to do almost anything (for the moment) rather than make everyone in the room hungry for his hide.

Because of its urgency, intervention demands that you be armed with the most important, basic information, and that you deliver this ammunition convincingly in the shortest period of time. Fortunately, the tools you need are relatively quick to learn and easy to apply.

Getting the Message Across

To intervene effectively, several things are necessary: You must get the dependent's attention. You must show her that you really care about her and really want to hear her side. You must demonstrate that you know the hidden truth and that what you say is factual and nonnegotiable. And you must convince the person to agree to accept specific help before you end the intervention.

The following four-step process can help you accomplish that in a matter of minutes. The steps are easy to remember as you go though them, because each begins with a letter that forms the word CARE:

Step 1: Confronting
Step 2: Affirming
Step 3: Responding
Step 4: Enacting

These four steps can be used by anyone to conduct any intervention.

STEP 1. CONFRONTING

Whoever has been selected to chair the intervention should welcome the dependent into the room and then tell the dependent why you are all there—the chemical dependency problem. Most conversations begin with a question or a statement, but in an intervention you do neither. In an emotional situation, either will bring about an argument. Something else is needed in here to get the dependent's attention and prove that this conversation is different, that you are being honest and open and asking the other person to do the same. You do this by sharing your honest concerns and feelings about the dependent and the dependency.

Family/Community Example: (*Ed*) Mayline, we're here because we love you and care about you. The people in this room all have something important that they would like to tell you. We ask only that you allow everyone to speak and, at the end, make whatever comments you wish. (*Joe*) I love you, honey. You are the brightest, most exciting, most loving woman I've ever known. But you have a chemical dependency problem. We can't ignore it any longer. You forget things, like eating or how to back out the car. Last week you totaled Jack's bike and almost Jack. (*Ellen*) Mom, you never go out anymore. All you do is drink and sleep. I can't even talk to you. (*Mark*) You're a good-looking woman but lately you've let yourself go to hell. (*Dr.*

Andrews) You're in pretty serious physical condition, Mayline. I'm really concerned.

Employer Example: (*Bill*) Mike, we're here because we care. Man, you are one of the finest journeymen we've ever had. But you obviously have a problem. You've missed 22 days of work this year. You're late almost daily. Your productivity has fallen off dramatically, according to these reports. (*Mack*) Man, you used to be one of our best crew. Last week, after disappearing for a while, you lost the Cooke and the Fuller jobs. We lost time and money we can't make up. Do you want to tell us what's going on or do we need to refer you for an assessment—you know the company policies.

Friends' Example: (*Cassy*) Donna, we're here because we all love you like a sister. You're the best friend I've got. You have more brains and imagination than anyone I've ever met. But you're out of control. Maybe you can't see it, but everyone else can. (*Wendy*) You've been my dearest friend for years. Since that party at Moe's, remember? We've had so many good times. We all party, but when the party is over, we stop. You keep going and going and going 'til it's oblivion. Then you're no party to be around, for sure. (*Sherry*) You're a kind person, but lately you wall yourself up in your room with your drugs and are downright bitchy. You're not yourself anymore. This thing has got you by the throat.

Professional Example: (*Art*) Joe, this is B. J. from New Way Center. We've asked him here because we're all worried about you. We think you have a chemical dependency problem. (*B. J., Interventionist*) Art, Sue, John and Jack called me because they have some very important things they want to tell you. If it is all right, I would ask only that you let them all speak first and then, at the end, respond. (*John*) Joe, you always were a man I could trust, a man of your word. But lately you have no end to the excuses and the lies. You swore four different times never to touch cocaine again, and each time broke your promise. (*Jack*) I've always had great faith in you. But lately it's all hot air. You made such big promises and were so productive for the first year, it sort of made up for the next three. Last week you "borrowed" petty cash without leaving a slip. I hear that's not the first time. (*Jerry*) Jack knows about the cocaine. I stepped in on you in the bathroom about two months ago. You didn't see me. (*Sue*) I told them about the piano. It's ridiculous. You've hocked everything that's worth anything. What's next? The kids? You're a crazy man. You never sleep. You can't sit still enough to listen. You almost knocked Joey out when he called you a doper, a ten-year-old kid! You're so paranoid you have wire-tap detectors on the telephones!

As we stated before, it is best to do the intervention with other people. It is almost impossible for an abuser to refute "corroborated testimony."

After you have effectively confronted, the dependent's response will come quickly. Depending on reaction style, it may be yelling, crying, rationalizing or withdrawing:

Yelling: "Who the hell are you to tell me what my problem is? None of you are saints! And you're wrong. I don't use any more than anyone else. If you are serious, you're going to have to try to prove it in court!"

Crying: "You don't understand. You are so hard on me. Why don't you all just leave me alone? You never gave a damn before this!"

Rationalizing: "Come off it! Look at you all. You'd drive anyone to drink! Do you think it's easy trying to support this family and do business on the lousy expense account you give me? I'd have burned out a long time ago if I couldn't veg-out once in a while!"

Withdrawing: "Apparently it doesn't matter what I say. You all obviously have your little agendas together. Go ahead. It's not my video."

Of course, these defenses hold as much beef broth as cheesecloth. Regardless of the dependent's response, you have already accomplished two things:

1. The dependent realizes he's met his Waterloo and he can't get away with it anymore.

2. He knows he can't escape the room and his only hope is to talk or act his way out. And he'll try.

No matter how much anger the addict expresses, the intervenors must remain calm, talk slowly and evenly and convey their caring concern. This will diffuse the anger.

STEP 2. AFFIRMING

This step requires that we affirm the person by listening—verbally and nonverbally—to what she says. When the dependent counterattacks with her heavy defenses, we may unconsciously try to defend ourselves by not hearing her or closing off our body language. Consciously, we want to listen. But if it is painful or threatening, we unconsciously try to shut her off (which is exactly what she wants, and she'll try to achieve it with anything she has!). We may say that we want an honest and open dialogue, but nonverbally we communicate the opposite message. Therefore, we must change our nonverbal communication to show that we are listening and intend to stick it out.

Studies show that when we speak, no matter what we say, over 85% of what we communicate (the meaning of what we are trying to say) rests in our nonverbal actions. These include body language, gestures, facial expressions, posture and especially eye contact. An easy way to remember how to communicate nonverbally is through SOBER listening, focusing on getting the person straight and sober.

SOBER LISTENING

S = Square shoulders (shows responsibility, your ability to bear the weight of the dependent's honesty)

O = Open arms (shows openness—a willingness to allow in what the dependent is saying)

B = Breathing (deeply and evenly to relax yourself as well as the dependent as you speak)

E = Eye contact (shows that the dependent has your full attention)

R = Relaxed posture (shows that you are comfortable in the situation and relaxes the dependent)

The second part of the affirming step is to prove to the dependent that you have really listened. This part of the affirmation process is based on one simple principle:

To get a person to listen, really listen to what we have to say, we must first listen fully to them and prove it!

We do this by repeating or mirroring exactly what the dependent just said as best we can, whether or not we believe, accept or understand it. In this way, we affirm the person by proving that we heard exactly what he or she said.

Example: So, Mayline, you say that if everyone were easier to live with, if there weren't so many crises in your life, you wouldn't need to pop pills and martinis to cope with it all.

By repeating what the other person has just said, you prove that you have listened. You restate part of his or her comments in your own words. This does not mean that you agree, only that you have really listened.

The other person's response will probably be one of genuine surprise. Moreover, the person will get a chance to hear his or her own point of view objectively (and it may not sound so great when someone else says it!).

The third part of the affirming step is to tell them again that they are important and worth sticking your neck out to help. Depending on their reaction style, they might want others to see their worth in their power or leadership, their performance, their ability to care or their intellect. Affirm the worth that is important to them and communicate that they stand to lose it all to a chemical dependency.

Example: Joe, if we really didn't care, we wouldn't have stuck behind you this far. You're a good person and you have a good brain, but it's all screwed up. You've got to clean it up.

In summary, you try to achieve three things in the Affirming step:

1. Show by your actions and body language that you are sincere and care about the dependent.
2. Acknowledge something the dependent has said by restating it in your own words, before using it to support what you have to say and driving home the chemical dependency problem.
3. Verbally reaffirm their personal worth to others.

The dependent will respond to your affirmation with another form of defense, usually defiance, defensiveness, bartering or rationalizing. This is important, because the dependent is beginning to really listen to you. (He wants to hear those affirmations!) You listen to what he has to say. When he finishes and awaits your response, when his ears are wide open after your last affirmations, bring out the heavy artillery.

STEP 3. RESPONDING

You do not put down, humiliate, ridicule or judge the dependent. You tell him he has a disease, and you present the facts, one right after another. Elaborate on them. Remember in this confrontation that your opponent is the disease—demonstrated by his denial. You attack the denial, not the person. You demonstrate the utmost care and concern for the dependent.

Some facts will register harder than others depending on what that person values most: her power and possessions, his reputation, her family and friends or his brain. If you know what is important, focus your attention on facts related to that area and use the others for support.

Example: John, you say that your family is the most important thing in the world to you, but look at them! You have a fourteen-year-old who wants to run off with her boyfriend to find some sanity, an eight-year-old that's turned into Rosemary's baby in the classroom and a wife whose sole companionship in life is the salesclerk at Bloomingdale's!

It is in Step 3 that the other people attending the intervention take over the intervention. Invite each person to take a turn to share their experiences and feelings. Ask the dependent to wait until the person has had a turn to speak before responding. Each person tells his point of view, sticks to the facts, then adds personal feelings. Most often the chemically dependent person has lied to himself about how others really feel, and the combination of facts and feelings (each person's own) can come as a great shock.

Example: Mom, I don't love you. I wish I did. I really try. Remember that time I bought you a sweatshirt? You said it didn't fit. The real reason is you can't say "Thank you" to anyone. Everything I do is nothing to you. I hate you for what you've done to us. Dad doesn't come home anymore. Why should he? I don't want any of my friends to see the way we live. You don't care what happens as long as everyone leaves you alone to get marinated.

Example: Joe, look. This is a chart of the "Stages of Dependency" showing how the disease progresses. Look how many checks are on it. It looks like you're somewhere between **Stage III** and **IV**. I care about you. But, man, I really can't handle this anymore. There are other people I'm responsible for. I've done as much as I can. You have a disease. It's not your fault, but, buddy, it's sure not mine either. It's time to do something about it. Now.

If the dependent tries to argue, give a rational response ("Carey is mad") and again ask the dependent to hold his comments until everyone has had a turn, and move on to another person, who adds more evidence and further builds the web. (To prepare, read the typical arguments and responses in Chapter 12!)

In summary, you try to do only one thing in Step 3: convince the person that the evidence of a dependency is clear. Everyone knows, and no one is going to take it any longer.

The dependent's response to Step 3 is usually one of giving up, although sometimes it is only an act just to get the heat off. Whichever it is, the giving up can be expressed in several different forms: frustration, resentment, helplessness or cynicism. This is your cue to enact a closure.

STEP 4. ENACTING

To be effective, the intervention must end with an action— not a promise or a good intention. You must enact a closure. Chemical dependency is cunning, baffling and powerful. No matter how much the chemically dependent person really wants to recover and how sincere her promises, the disease will overrule them as soon as she is left alone with it.

The chairman takes over here. The intervention objective is to use the information from the intervention to get the person to commit to a specific recovery program, and then to enforce the decision. One useful tool is the Recovery Ultimatum—the ultimate force of the entire confrontation.

The Recovery Ultimatum is used to close the intervention. It is the final statement before the dependent is asked for his decision—it forces "enactment."

In short, the fourth step will :

1. Summarize the facts, relating them to the urgency to begin recovery.

2. Present the specific Recovery Objective (or the treatment options).

3. State the Recovery Ultimatum and the means of enforcement.

Example: (*Jim*) John, you say your family is important to you and you see it is going to hell. You want to do something about it. We have contacted someone in AA who will come by to talk to you this afternoon, if you agree, and take you to a meeting tonight. If that doesn't work for you, Serenity Street will take you as an in-patient on Friday. We've worked out the insurance arrangements. (*Rose*) Honey, the kids and I are really behind you, and we want to see you get well. We have so much life ahead of us. It's not too late, but if you don't commit to a recovery program today, it's over for us. I have round-trip tickets to Mom's for me and the kids. We're leaving tomorrow for three weeks. We'll know by then whether we have a reason to come back here. (*Jim*) She means it, and we're all behind her. What's your decision?

Usually one Recovery Ultimatum is sufficient, although in a community intervention, two or three might be appropriate. The most powerful are the ones that offer the choice between a reward for recovery and a severe penalty for further abuse. Here are some additional examples:

- We need you in the band. You're a brother, man. There are no limits to what we can do together if we all support each other. But if this shit isn't killing you, it's sure killing us. You get help today and we'll all stick behind you, man, whatever is required. Otherwise, it's over. History.
- If you get help today and you stay clean and sober, I have an agreement here for the financing that will help us turn the company around. If you don't, I'm tearing this up and closing down immediately.
- You are my daughter. You have given me my happiest and my saddest moments. I want to see you grow to be everything you can be. I'll always love you, but I won't watch you die. You get help today or you find somewhere else to live.

No Bargaining

An intervention is not the place for bargaining, promising or negotiating with the addict. ("Let me try to cut down on my own. If I can't, then I'll get help. I swear.") After all, you'll be up against a slicker-tongued salesman than ever graced a parking lot full of used Corvairs! Remember, the addict is dealing from desperation.

Recovery demands total abstinence and outside help. Go for broke. It's an all-or-nothing proposition. No compromises.

Summarize the major points: We're here because we care. You have a fatal disease. Without help, it gets worse, never better. You can't do it by yourself. You've proven that already. Help is available now. We're all behind you. Everything is set. Your bags are packed. Unless you have any good reasons why you shouldn't, this is it. Let's go.

Don't accept a put-off or delay. Things always appear differently in the morning.

In Conclusion

The intervention process is a simple one: Confront the disease as the problem. Affirm with care and concern (verbally and nonverbally). Respond to excuses and defenses with hard facts. Enact a specific action to get help.

Remember these keys:

- Pick a neutral location.
- Surprise the dependent.
- Have others present.
- Communicate care, concern and the facts.
- Give the ultimatum.
- Do not bargain.

Some people have found it helpful to review a checklist of the characteristics of a dependency with the dependent while others are present. Two such checklists appear in Appendices E and F: "Are You Alcoholic?" and "Are You Drug Addicted?"

NOTICE!

Never put yourself or others in physical danger!

If the dependent has demonstrated a tendency toward violence, depression or suicide due to the drugs or his/her nature, take these precautions:

1. Get professional help from a mental health clinic or licensed treatment center before intervening.

2. Never intervene in the person's home or on his/her turf. Rather, locate neutral ground.

3. Always have at least one other person present.

4. Always convey your personal concern and care for the person while you explain what the person used to be like, how he/she has changed as a result of alcohol or drugs, and how you feel about it.

5. Leave out the bottom line/Recovery Ultimatum and urge the person to get help.

6. If the person tells you to go to hell, say that you need to take care of yourself and must make the necessary adjustments in your life. Then do so.

Anticipating the Dependent's Response

♦

"Cobras have fangs, skunks have fumes, elephants have weight and tigers have jowls. If you don't know the beast you are confronting, you may find yourself hissed at, pissed at, trampled or eaten alive."

—Wise old interventionist

Differences in Reaction Style

Although the four-step CARE intervention will proceed well with little other information, it's even more effective if you know something about the dependent's basic way of responding—his style of acting.

Researchers on type differences say that people can be categorized into four general styles based on how they act, react and interact with the world. To avoid complicated clinical terms, we call the four types ActionStyles. In working with counselors, patients and their families over the last seven years, we discovered several things about type differences that have helped everyone involved to better understand and support the recovery process. Much of this information is valuable in an intervention—especially in predicting the dependent's reaction.

Each of the four types, or ActionStyles, has its own perspective, needs or objectives in life, and preferred way of achieving them. Not surprisingly, each tends to seek out drugs for different reasons.

Before the addiction took over, the dependent person relied on a certain chemical (or chemicals) to help him achieve these specific objectives. In every case, the person's objectives are now being lost or destroyed because of the addiction.

And this is the message that communicates the strongest in an intervention.

The four ActionStyles are: Harmonizers, Organizers, Performers and Explorers. They are easy to remember since the first letter of each spells HOPE.

Because each style represents a differing set of values, each will naturally conflict with the others unless there is an understanding of each other's perspective and how it applies in his everyday reasoning.

(Note: In the following descriptions, jobs are given as examples to help you visualize the type of person often associated with them. Don't try to match them with the job of the dependent. ActionStyles can be found in any job.)

HARMONIZERS

Harmonizers are the group workers of society—the people who need people. People are their reason for existence, and harmony is their objective in life. You'll always find them preoccupied with others. They place a great emphasis on personal growth and character development, especially their own. They may be outward-focused, such as the exciting leaders of team projects, social groups or community or business efforts; or they may be inward-focused and enjoy writing or interpreting various philosophies. Harmonizers frequently get so involved in the problems of others that they neglect their own problems, often failing to take care of themselves.

Whether personnel directors, bartenders or elementary

ACTIONSTYLE PROFILER®

	HARMONIZER	ORGANIZER	PERFORMER	EXPLORER
PRIORITY	People	Purpose	Fun	Ideas
INITIATIVE	Discovery	Harmony	Order	Pleasure
METHOD	Caring	Structure	Spontaneity	Logic
DRIVE	Sharing	Belonging	Experiencing	Seeking
DISPOSITION	Sensitive	Controlled	Charismatic	Distant
GREATEST DISLIKE	Conflict	Disorganization	Routines	Restrictions
GREATEST FEAR	Abandonment	Powerlessness	Insignificance	Illogic/ridicule
HOW TO MOTIVATE	Approval	Responsibility	Challenges	Freedom
HOW TO INTERVENE	Losing love	Losing control	Losing freedom	Losing mind
HOW TO REWARD	Appreciation	Authority	Material goods	Respect
HOW TO DIRECT	Give affection	Give rules	Give alternatives	Give reason

school teachers, they are intense feelers of not only their own but everyone else's pain or discomfort.

Harmonizers rely on chemicals initially to cope with disharmony, to dull the pain of rejection or a lost relationship, to escape a sense of loss, personal failure or guilt, or simply to socialize and get close to other people. They become addicted to a wide range of chemicals that can lower inhibitions and dull the senses, especially alcohol, marijuana, hypnotics and tranquilizers.

The best way to reach Harmonizers is to show how their chosen chemical has hurt other people, destroyed relationships with family and friends, caused resentments among co-workers and is destroying a very special person (themselves).

Most importantly, the intervention must demonstrate caring and tell how recovery can bring about reconciliation, harmony and personal growth, but only if the Harmonizer can get help now before the disease progresses too far.

Although shocked and embarrassed, Harmonizers stay through an intervention to try to please certain people in the room as well as to witness the love and concern of others that they do not feel for themselves.

ORGANIZERS

Organizers are the power players in life. They have the ability to push buttons, pull levers and get people together to produce. The bottom line is most important to them. They value stability and belonging to an organization or group. Because they are usually so responsible, people put them in positions of great responsibility (and if they don't, Organizers tend to assume those positions anyway). Family, company and material things are important to them. As managers or moms, they have innate leadership qualities, unless obsession with their power, or lack of it, makes them dominating. Whether energetic and people-oriented administrators, leaders and representatives, or stable and quiet overseers (such as physicians, office workers, record-keepers and medical professionals), Organizers are particularly susceptible to stimulant addiction, especially cocaine, as well as to alcoholism developed during friendly socializing, while "moving and shaking" or when trying to cope with the uncopable.

Organizers use alcohol and drugs primarily to feel powerful, to overcome feelings of inadequacy or to have a sense of control over the uncontrollable.

The best way to reach Organizers during an intervention is to show how their chosen chemical has made them lose all their personal power, control and everything important to them, and how recovery will help them get it all back.

Organizers are humiliated and disrupted by the intervention, but soon find the need to belong and to reestablish control as compelling motives to stay.

PERFORMERS

Performers are recognition seekers. Where the Organizer's emphasis is the product or the bottom line (what's it all mean?), the Performer's emphasis is the action—the doing of it. They may be focused on the outside world and be exciting and energetic, always promoting or entertaining, such as politicians, actors or athletes. Or they may be focused on the world inside them and be quieter doers, like artists and artisans, always using their hands. The Performer's great thrill is in the experience, the moment, the actual performance and the fact that they are doing it themselves. They are so caught up in their own projects that they often seem oblivious to the needs of others. They are especially concerned about money, appearance and health—all of which they use adeptly to experience life to its fullest. Whether sales persons, elementary teachers, dynamic moms or football stars, Performers place the highest value on how others think of them—their image or identity. They used their chemicals to "party," to be the center of attention, to relax, to experience the ultimate sensations and to be regarded popularly as good at what they do.

Performers become addicted to a wide range of drugs because they rely on them for the sensation they give. They are particularly susceptible to those that give a sense of euphoria (narcotics, sedative-hypnotics), new experiences (hallucinogens) or competency and peak performance (cocaine), as well as alcohol to feel good and relax—a dependency developed over years of drinking with others.

The best way to reach Performers is to show how their chosen chemical has made them lose their health, looks and

Healthy...

Harmonizers

Harmonizers are people who need people and who strive to create harmony. Their goal in life is "to become" and to help make the world around them a better place. Harmonizers tend to feel intensely. They are dramatically affected by their own or another's pain and are sought by others for nurturing, counseling and guidance.

Organizers

Organizers need to belong. Organizations are important to them. They are concerned with power and procedure, both expecting and respecting the authority to which they've pledged allegiance. Practical and efficient, they have the uncanny ability to bring minds and means together, take care of others, maintain order and get things done.

Performers

Performers need to be free. They tend to be dynamic and spontaneous, seek out action and live for the moment. They dislike rules and routine, avoid facing problems or looking at the past. They are creative risk takers who look forward to the unusual, land on their feet, and have an ability to focus on the now–the process–while keeping an open mind.

Explorers

Explorers demand logic. Theirs is a constant search for knowledge and an intense self-criticism. Even their play is work, always looking for ways to improve things. Seeing possibilities others don't and indifferent to authority unless there is merit, they are ever focused on the future and refuse to waste time on rules and routines.

Dependent...

Harmonizers

Chemically dependent Harmonizers can be both lavish and miserly, harsh and remorseful, emotional and cold, organized and frenzied, blaming *use* on a trauma. They people-please, manipulate, are passive-aggressive, insecure, and obsessed with a cause or another's love or infidelity. Depressed, they deny, lie, isolate, are paranoid and suicidal.

Organizers

Chemically dependent Organizers are often obsessed with power and position, use careless force, refuse compromise, and self-justify with anger, denial, blame, distortions, rejection and workaholism. They imagine infidelity and conspiracy, become selfish, belligerent, arrogant and often violent, relying on "net worth" to prove their self-worth.

Performers

Chemically dependent Performers can be egotistical, self-obsessed, promiscuous, irresponsible moving targets, using promises, blame and procrastination to avoid confrontation. Exciting and bizarre, their obsession with money, material comfort and pleasure can lead to distortion, manipulation, theft, desertion, compulsive spending and "geographics."

Explorers

Chemically dependent Explorers can be isolating, arrogant, self-driven, paranoid, insensitive and manipulating. Always obsessed with some project or goal (the ship coming in), they use brilliant logic to deceive selves and others and can be both workaholic and lethargic, procrastinating of major responsibilities and prone to sudden disappearances.

ability to perform, as well as the appreciation and admiration of the people they admire, and how they can get it all back if they can get help now.

Although Performers are stunned and threatened by the intervention, they are drawn to the attention and the challenge it affords, as well as to the obvious teamwork.

EXPLORERS

Explorers are the critical thinkers of society—the inventors, designers, innovators, social reformers and engineers. Always looking for a better way, their primary concern is logical merit, and their most valued possession is their own intellect. They may be externally focused, such as energetic inventors (always coming up with a better idea) and directors (always developing a new plan), or internally focused, such as systems analysts, scientists and graphic designers.

Their approach to life is both theoretical and practical, an endless pursuit of the answer to "What if?" Valuing personal freedom over rules of conduct, Explorers are not afraid to test their mental limits. For some this includes experimenting with chemicals, as long as they believe they will cause no permanent damage to their brains.

Explorers initially use chemicals to trigger mental processes, believing that their thinking flows faster with a little help, or to achieve cohesiveness when feelings interfere with thinking. For these reasons they are especially susceptible to hallucinogens (mental exploration), marijuana (mental freedom), and a wide range of depressants, including alcohol, to calm the nerves.

Explorers can be reached best by showing how their chosen chemical is interfering with their brain function, how their actions have been illogical, how the very thing they hope to gain by using their chemical is being destroyed because of it. The intervention must proceed logically from cause to effect to solution to action.

Although feeling incensed, restricted and irritated, Explorers tend to stay through the intervention because they find the logic of the intervention and the information about dependency intriguing.

It is important to remember that addiction makes a chemical the priority in each person's life regardless of reaction style. But the addicted person does not know that yet. He still believes his chemical is somehow tied in with achieving that objective. Your role is to show him that the opposite is true: that his chemical is defeating his objective.

Recognizing Differences

Obviously, no matter how intelligent or creative any type may be, an addictive chemical brings out the worst in a person. Compare the descriptions of the Healthy and the Dependent version of each type.

Another way of looking at this comparison might be as the kind of recovery: Before (Dependent) and After (Healthy). It should give you a glimpse of what the real person can be like without the dependency.

The "Healthy-Dependent" chart (pages 124–25) will help you see some of the major differences between the ActionStyles.

Note that each has different needs, priorities, fears and dislikes; and each responds best to a different way of being instructed, motivated, guided and rewarded. By recognizing these differences, you can be even more effective in reaching the dependent.

Identifying the unique differences between yourself and the dependent can help you understand your own reactions as the intervention takes place.

Some people may not seem to fit snugly in one category or another. That is because we have the capability for all ActionStyles in ourselves. But one style dominates how we prefer to think and act, and is usually a major clue to our inner priorities.

Your Turn

Try now to identify what is most important to the person on whom you are intervening and build a strategy around that person's highest priority in life. By recognizing people's inherent differences in ActionStyle, you gain one more important tool in a caring and effective intervention—one tailored especially to your dependent's needs.

Intervening with CARE

	HARMONIZER (Group Worker) Needs People	ORGANIZER (Dominating Doer) Needs Power	PERFORMER (Recognition Seeker) Needs Dignity	EXPLORER (Critical Thinker) Needs Logic
Step 1: Confronting	We're here, ___ because you have a serious problem. We care too much to watch...	You have a serious problem, ___. You know it. You're completely out of control.	We know you have a serious problem. Everyone does. But do you?	___, you have a serious problem that can't be ignored any longer.
(Probable reaction)	*(MARTYRDOM) If you would leave me alone, I could handle it. Don't worry about me. I'll be fine if you just leave me alone.*	*(AGGRESSION) What do you mean? How can anyone perform with these people and all the pressures I'm under. It's your fault...*	*(MORTIFICATION) It isn't that bad. So what if I party hard? I like a good time. You're really making a big thing out of nothing.*	*(OUTRAGE) What I do with my life is my business, not yours! There are plenty of people out there with a worse problem.*
Step 2: Affirming	You have a disease. Every day people like you die trying to get on top of it alone. We want you to get professional help.	You have every right to be angry. I'd be if I were you. You've worked too hard to see everything you've built go to hell.	We're here because, frankly, ___ your partying isn't a party anymore. It's turning you into a fool, a village idiot.	I'm afraid you've made it our business. You have a disease and you need professional help. You're in pretty bad shape.
(Probable reaction)	*(BARTERING) It's not that bad. I'll be okay. All I need is a little co-operation.*	*(DEFIANCE) I don't need you telling me what my problems are...*	*(DEFENSIVENESS) I'm not hurting anyone! So I need to blow off a little steam.*	*(RATIONALIZING) I haven't done anything wrong. I haven't hurt anyone.*

Step 3: **R**ESPONDING	That's what we're doing. You have a family disease. The problem is that it's not only killing you, it's hurting everyone around you. (Give examples.)	You have a disease. It's robbing you of your power, your family, home, and money, your health, career and future. (Give examples).	You have a disease, ___. It gets worse, never better. It's robbing you of friends, family, your looks and your dignity! (Give examples.)	If you're so smart how come you're here? You have a great mind but this disease is making you lose it. You've made bad decisions. (Give examples.)
(Probable reaction)	(HELPLESSNESS) So what am I supposed to do?	(FRUSTRATION) So what are you trying to say?	(RESENTMENT) So what do you expect me to do?	(CYNICISM) You have all the answers. What do I do?
Step 4: **E**NACTING	There is a program that can help. It involves other people in the same situation you're in—a way that by helping each other you can help yourselves. (Volunteer) is here to take you to get help. You hurt. We hurt. It's time to put an end to it all. Aren't you sick and tired of being sick and tired? We are. What's your decision?	You've become a slave to a stupid chemical. But you can win your freedom back. You can get back power over your life, if you want it. You have two choices. You can die a slow death and be remembered as a guy who lost it all. Or you can get help tonight. (Volunteer) will take you. I think you can lick it, with help. But do you?	You can change things but it won't be easy. You've got everything to gain if you get help now, and lots of people believe you can do it. We do. You've faced tough things before, ___. If anyone can beat this thing, you can, with help. (Volunteer) will take you to get that help right now. The rest is up to you. What do you say?	This kind of chemical dependency gets worse, never better. You have all the signs of an addict. The only possible chance you have is to get to people who know about this stuff and to do what you have to do to control it. (Volunteer) will explain the program to you and take you to get help tonight. Any questions?

The chart on pages 128–29 demonstrates how to apply ActionStyle to "Intervening with CARE." Select the style that is closest to that of your dependent. Read down the columns and see how the conversation would logically progress through the four steps: Confronting, Affirming, Responding and Enacting.

Especially note how the basic need or objective of each style can be brought into the intervention.

INTERVENING ON A HARMONIZER

The intervention for Harmonizers focuses most attention on their need for people. The first step, Confronting, emphasizes the group's care and concern for the Harmonizer (who feels that nobody cares and secretly is overwhelmed and embarrassed by the attention of the group). Harmonizers know how to take care of others but can't reach out for help for themselves. They feel that doing so lets everyone else down and erodes others' faith in them. When threatened, this nurturer responds with noble martyrdom. Making others feel guilty is the Harmonizer's main weapon. ("Don't worry. I'll be fine.")

Note that the second step, Affirming, drives home the main point and relates it to the Harmonizer's value of life itself. "You have a disease. Every day people like you die trying to get on top of it alone. We want you to get professional help." Of course, the Harmonizer will agree with the group to keep the harmony, but doesn't believe that life is possible without the chemical and will try to put the intervenor off using passive blame and bartering: "All I need is a little cooperation." The Harmonizer is trying to gain control of the intervention by offering compromises, backed up with excuses and promises.

In the third step, Responding, the chairman again drives home the point, picking up on the part of the Harmonizer's defense that can lead into the tough love segment of the intervention: "Cooperation is why we're here. You have a family disease . . . it's hurting everyone around you." Give examples that start off with each person's love and true feeling for the Harmonizer, their hurt and disappointment, and their hope for the future. This is striking right at the heart, for the last thing a Harmonizer wants is to hurt other people. There is no possible response from the dependent but helpless agreement, because the Harmonizer is completely disarmed.

Finally, in the fourth and final step, Enacting, the group offers a way that the Harmonizer can help him or herself and many others. They back it up with an enforceable Ultimatum. The Harmonizer is left with no choice but to cooperate, all the while feeling that he or she is loved and is an important and vital person in the lives of the people in the room.

INTERVENING ON AN ORGANIZER

The intervention for Organizers focuses heaviest attention on their need for power. The first step, Confronting, emphasizes the Organizer's total loss of control (a fact that is secretly gnawing at the dependent daily as he or she tries desperately to regain it and continues to lose it). Naturally, when threatened, the power-player responds with aggression (use of force is an Organizer's main weapon) and with blame (to cover up for the loss of power).

Note that the second step, Affirming, drives home the point and relates to the Organizer's value of material possessions: "You've worked too hard to see it all go to hell!" Of course, the Organizer agrees with that but doesn't want to admit it, so will try to put the intervenor off with the John Wayne approach: "I don't need you telling me my problems." The Organizer is trying to gain control of the intervention.

In the third step, Responding, the chairman again drives home the point: "You have a disease. It's robbing you of your power, your family, your home . . ." (everything important to this person). There is no possible response from the dependent but to agree.

Finally, in the fourth and final step, Enacting, the group offers a way that the Organizer can regain control. They back it up with an enforceable ultimatum and repeat that the decision is his to make. The Organizer, recognizing his powerlessness to control the dependency, is fully aware of his power of choice. He has two options. The choice is his to make!

INTERVENING ON A PERFORMER

The intervention for Performers focuses strongest attention on their need for dignity. The first step, Confronting, emphasizes that everyone else is aware of the problem (a fact that the

Performer successfully camouflaged for a while, using all the "wires and mirrors" of a magic show). When threatened, this recognition seeker most often responds with mortification—shock, denial, justification and an attempt to reassure, with charm or humor, that nothing is really wrong. Whatever tack the Performer uses, it is usually quite a convincing performance—after all, this person is desperate.

Note that the second step, Affirming, hits on the Performer's value of socializing and being noticed in a positive way by others, but that the reaction is quite the opposite of what the Performer sought: "Frankly, your partying isn't a party anymore. It's turning you into a fool, a village idiot." Of course, the Performer will care but doesn't want to admit it, so will try to put the intervenor off with defensiveness. "I'm not hurting anyone. So I need to blow off a little steam!" Again, the Performer is trying to gain some compassion and make use of the spotlight to escape. You may see some fancy footwork and brilliant arguments, such as now is the worst time to go to treatment because of some tremendous thing that is about to happen, etc.

In the third step, Responding, the chairman again drives home the point: "You have a disease. It gets worse, never better. It's robbing you of your dignity." Appearance is very important, so references to how the dependency is affecting the Performer's looks, health and freedom are also effective—all the things that are important to this person. There is no possible response from the dependent but to agree.

Finally, in the fourth and final step, Enacting, the intervenors offer a way that the Performer can regain popularity, dignity and "personal power." They back it up with an enforceable ultimatum. The Performer is left with no choice but to cooperate, while maintaining dignity and a sense of personal freedom. ("You've faced tough things before. . . . If anyone can beat this, you can, with help.")

INTERVENING ON THE EXPLORER

The intervention for Explorers focuses greatest attention on their need for logic. The first step, Confronting, emphasizes that a serious problem has been ignored (nothing grabs an Explorer's attention faster than pointing out a problem others see that he or she may have overlooked). Naturally, when threatened, the critical thinker responds with indignity and outrage, relying on a logical argument. Subjective use of "facts" is an Explorer's main weapon. ("My life is my business, not yours! There are plenty of people out there with a worse problem!")

To continue the intervention, the chairman must gain the Explorer's respect. Note how the second step, Affirming, accomplishes this by picking apart the Explorer's defense statement, logically diffusing it: "You've made it our business. . . ." Talk about the family, job, finances. Bring the Affirming to a logical conclusion. "You have a disease. . . . It always gets worse. . . . You need help now. . . . You're in bad shape." Of course, you may want to show how faulty his logic is: "Sure, some people are worse than you. They're bankrupt, in jails and on rubber sheets. And if you put your mind to it, you can be as smart as they are!" Logically, the Explorer will agree with that but doesn't want to admit it so will try to put the intervenor off: "I haven't done anything wrong" (e.g., "I've never been out of control. You've never seen me drunk" or "I've never had a DUI"). Again, the Explorer is trying to gain control of the intervention through the use of that powerful sense of logic.

In the third step, Responding, the chairman again drives home the point that the Explorer is losing the thing he or she values most in life—his or her brain: "If you're so smart, how come you're here? You have a great mind, but this disease is making you lose it. You've made bad decisions." (Give specific examples. If the Explorer argues with them, nod and continue with more examples.) Eventually, there is no possible response from the dependent but to agree, which is done cynically to try to save face. "You have all the answers. What do I do?" What the dependent really means is, "God, maybe there really is a way out."

Finally, in the fourth and final step, Enacting, the group offers a way that the Explorer can regain mental control and back it up with an enforceable ultimatum. The Explorer can only cooperate, all the while valuing the right to make the logical choice!

Remember, if the CARE is there, all else will follow.

Understanding the Mind Games

◆

"The committee was always meeting inside my head."
"Yeah. That's the nice part about being schizophrenic.
You're never really alone."

There are two minds to consider at this point—that mish-mashed, red-buttoned dashboard of the addict and your own mission control system. We've already reviewed what is happening biochemically and how it affects the dependent's thinking. But while his brain is medicated, yours is caught up in the emotional cross fire.

A Positive Attitude

Like all the challenges of life, attitude is everything. If you are preoccupied with the possible failure, set your goals too high, level the guillotine of perfectionism at yourself, you will surely achieve some degree of personal defeat, at least in your own mind.

If you expect to expose the problem and jumpstart the recovery process, hoping for the best and remembering that the outcomes are not in your hands, the chances are far better that you'll see real results.

Some call it the power of positive thinking. Actually, it is nothing more than your ability to show the chemically dependent person that at least one person believes there is hope. In the beginning, that is far more than even the addict can hope for.

No human being, least of all one in the depression of dependency, can see something positive in herself until someone else sees it first and points it out. (The same is true for both good and bad. Consider this the next time you see your teenagers—what do they see in your eyes when you look at them? Hope or despair? Appreciation or regret?)

One of the great advantages of self-help groups is the number of recovering people who look at the terrified addict entering the room, nod at him and smile, as if to say, "I've been there. But now I'm well. You're going to be okay, too." At their meetings, older AA members will often tell new ones, "Desperation got us here. Inspiration keeps us here."

In flying an airplane, novice aviators are taught that "attitude governs altitude." Attitude is the position assumed to achieve a certain effect.

When a pilot points the nose of the plane up and changes its attitude relative to the ground, the plane goes up and gains altitude. If the pilot points it down, it loses altitude, rapidly— right into the ground unless the pilot changes the attitude. People can defy gravity and make astounding things happen by being positive. So aim for the heavens. Go for it all.

Inside the Dysfunctional Family

If you are a member of the dependent's immediate family and feel emotional turmoil about the forthcoming intervention, there is good reason why. You have been living in a dysfunctional relationship. There are several behaviors that typically characterize the family of a chemically dependent person. To

ActionStyles® in the Dysfunctional Family

Role		Action	HARMONIZER	ORGANIZER	PERFORMER	EXPLORER
Baby	Cause concern	Irresponsibility	X	X	X	X
Chief Enabler	Responsibility	Covers up, holds family together	X	X		
Family Hero	Self-worth	Visible success, provides for others	X	X		X
Scapegoat	Distraction	Runs away, rebels, digs in, stubborn	X		X	X
Lost Child	Offer relief	Cut off, removed, covers up feelings	X	X		X
Mascot	Bring fun	Charm and humor	X		X	

survive, individual family members usually assume specific roles which interplay for different motives.

Throughout the last 20 years, much work has been done to identify the typical survival roles assumed by the different family members of the dependent (the co-dependents). Much of the credit goes to the workshops and books of Sharon Wegscheider and Virginia Satir. (See Bibliography.)

We found this knowledge invaluable in our work with families in treatment and recovery. Moreover, we soon discovered a strong correlation between the ActionStyles of the family members and the specific survival roles they had assumed. Harmonizers, Organizers, Performers or Explorers each have inherent character strengths and weaknesses which contribute to the behavior they assume in the dysfunctional family.

Baby: As the addiction goes out of control, family members silently pick up more and more responsibility, allowing the dependent to act as the demanding infant whom everyone tries to hide and protect and upon whom everyone waits hand and foot! The dependent soon realizes this and uses the situation to keep everyone else in tow. The Baby's role is to cause concern. Usually, it is the spouse or mate of the addict who assumes the role of parent. Obviously, mating problems develop—it's hard for a man to make love to his "mother" or a woman to her "father."

Addicts of all ActionStyles (Harmonizers, Organizers, Performers and Explorers) assume the role of Baby and selfishly act out feelings of aggression, grandiosity, charm and rigidity to cover up for pain, guilt, shame and fear. Harmonizer Babies tend to be alternately charmers and victims—real crybabies. Organizer Babies are most often demanding, possessive and vengeful. Performer Babies are likely to be spoiled brats, alternately entertaining and throwing tantrums. Explorer Babies are usually single-minded, insensitive and relentless. Addicts unconsciously use these Baby behaviors to keep the family off balance and preoccupied with meeting their needs.

Chief Enabler: The Chief Enabler is the person who feels most responsible for the welfare of the chemically dependent person. Usually, it is the spouse or mate or one of the parents, although in broken families it is not unusual to see one of the children assume this "adult" position. The role of the Chief Enabler is to provide responsibility. All family members enable to some extent, but the Chief Enabler's duty is to make everything seem normal to the outside world. The Chief Enabler acts out feelings of superresponsibility, manipulation, martyrdom and self-blame to cover up for hurt, anger, fear and guilt. Harmonizers (because of their concern for others and a natural desire to nurture) and Organizers (because of their need to have order, responsibility and unity) are ideally "set up" for the Chief Enabler role. Almost all persons we worked with who were identified as the Chief Enablers in their families turned out to be Organizers or Harmonizers in type testing.

Family Hero: This is the person who observes everything that is happening and feels responsible because he cannot turn the situation around, despite hard work and occupational success. The Hero's role is to provide the family with self-worth. He or she uses hard work, superresponsibility, independence and achievement to cover up for feelings of loneliness, hurt, confusion, failure and anger. Organizers (because they experience success in organizations of all types) and, to a lesser extent, Explorers (who take their work seriously and tend to remove themselves from emotional conflict) are perfect setups for the Family Hero role, which they almost always assume.

Scapegoat: This is the family member who gives up on everyone and everything and looks for "family" elsewhere, often seeking out radical pursuits. The role is to provide distraction to the family. Scapegoats use sullenness, defiance, rebellion and chemicals to cover up feelings of loneliness, anger, fear, hurt and rejection. Because they do not want to cope with pain, and tend to run at the first sign of trouble, Performers are ideally suited to the role of Scapegoat. If two children are of the same sex, and the Hero role is taken by one, the second will usually assume the Scapegoat role, especially if the two children are both Harmonizers.

Lost Child: This is the quiet member of the family who disappears into the woodwork, most often alone and quietly busy. Overlooked or taken for granted by the rest of the family, the role of the Lost Child is to provide relief (as the one person no one needs to worry about). Almost always the Lost Child is an Explorer, or, to a far lesser extent, the family's second or third Organizer or Harmonizer child. This member uses aloofness, rejection, independence and sometimes food to compensate for loneliness, anger, hurt and inadequacy.

Mascot: This is the person who brings a little laughter or charm into the family, using humor and entertainment to lighten a dismal atmosphere. No one looks inside to see that there is much below the surface. The role is to provide fun for the family. Mascots use clowning, displays, hyperactivity and appeal to cover up fear, insecurity, confusion and loneliness. No one is better suited for the role of Mascot than the Performer, who plays it to the hilt. If there are no Performers in the family, the role is most often assumed by a younger Harmonizer.

Understanding the roles that different people assume to survive in a dysfunctional family can help each person understand a little more clearly their conflicting emotions when faced with an intervention. This is the reason why a family recovery program is so very important. Such roles may offer temporary protection and security, but in the long run they stifle personal growth and erode us of our self-esteem.

Predictable Emotional Changes

Although you may feel somewhat nervous during the intervention, the dependent is as alert as a cat discovered on the chain link fence of a dog pound. If you think your antennae are up, imagine what he must be thinking.

Outward appearances are deceiving. Most addicts will try to fool you into thinking they are not taken aback by this gang-up of confronters ("You have simply made a mistake—I don't have a problem!).

Expect to witness some spectacular tap-dancing while he tries to make a quick exit. The dependent has developed an intricate life support system, and you are threatening to take it away. Survival without it seems utterly unthinkable.

When the full impact hits, the dependent will go through the same emotions that all human beings experience when they lose something vital—a loved one (through death or divorce), a home, business or job, etc. This process was first identified by Elisabeth Kübler-Ross in working with the terminally ill.

Just as when you cut your arm, it automatically begins a long but predictable healing process, the same is true of human emotions.

The physical wound will bleed, swell as the white blood cells fight infection, become numb, form a scab and finally lose its scab, revealing new skin. Similarly, emotions have their own step-by-step healing process, sometimes called "the grieving process."

The Healing/Grieving Process

In this process, a person first experiences DENIAL of the loss (refusing to admit that the problem or loss exists), then ANGER-FEAR (fighting the unalterable reality or running from it), followed by MANIPULATION (bartering with reality in order to get away with accepting a small part of the reality while refusing other parts), DEPRESSION (giving up on everyone and everything) and, finally, ACCEPTANCE (dealing with the reality and reorganizing one's life to go on).

Be prepared for these emotions and know that if you witness them in the dependent, things are going as they should.

Emotions are natural, normal and inevitable. The emotions connected with the healing process are vital and essential to recovery. No emotion is good or bad. It simply IS. How a person handles his or her own emotions can be good or bad.

Denial, the biggest roadblock, happens not only because the addict can't imagine living without the chemical, but also because the person's vision is so distorted that he cannot see the behavior you see.

The dependent's worst behavior probably occurred just prior to passing out, blacking out or checking out. The addict doesn't see the jerky, disjointed walk or hear the weird speech. From the inside, everything looks fine.

No alcoholic forms a connection between the disasters and the drinking. No coke addict connects the blow and the blow-ups. No grass addict connects the tuning out with the turning off. When stopped by a cop, they'll sincerely believe the reason for driving erratically was that the road was paved poorly, the tires were low or the steering mechanism on the car has too much "play."

It is natural for the addict to get mad that the problem was discovered and that he or she can never drink or use the "beloved" chemical again. If the person works through the anger and uses it to expose and examine the past, and turns the anger toward the chemical, that is healthy and good. If the person uses the anger to hurt someone or to go out on a roll, this is obviously not healthy.

As with physical healing, the emotional healing process must include all the steps. A person cannot skip over a step but must experience it in sequence. If one step is not worked through, the process cannot continue. If a wound continues to be angry and inflamed, gangrene sets in and an untimely death results. People stuck in anger are the ones that kill themselves or others.

Since all people who suffer a serious loss go through the emotional healing process, so do the family members—during the dependency *and* the recovery.

They, in fact, are losing a predictably unpredictable relationship with a chemically altered person. Recovery brings many changes.

Family members experience denial of the dependency (blaming it on other things), anger toward the dependent (blaming the dependent for all the problems), manipulation (covering up the dependency and repeatedly exacting unkept promises), depression (giving up, numbness or thoughts of suicide when all seems hopeless) and, finally, acceptance of the disease (doing what needs to be done for all to recover).

It is our experience that emotional healing involves a cycle. The first time through all the emotions, the majority of time is spent in DENIAL, with little or no time in ACCEPTANCE. The second time through, less time is spent in DENIAL, more in MANIPULATION and some in ACCEPTANCE.

Once a person achieves full acceptance, a quality recovery has taken place. The person goes on to live life with gratitude, patience and a new-found energy.

How to Respond to Typical Arguments

◆

"The best defense is a good offense."

—Vince Lombardi

Whether you realize it or not, in the addict's mind the intervenors have just declared war. Even before the first word of the intervention is fired, the dependent is on Red Alert. His adrenaline is pumping so fast he could switch off the lights and be gone before the room gets dark. But you've blocked the exits.

So expect the subject of your "unwarranted and inhuman" attack to launch a counteroffensive with the biggest verbal missiles in his arsenal. If he's any good at it, they'll land with an intensity that would make Nagasaki look like the spore-spray of a forest mushroom. After all, he thinks he's fighting for his survival.

Life without his drug is as inconceivable to the addict as surviving without oxygen.

The group will have to be prepared for this and well armed with iron-clad comebacks to all the addict's best shots. In fact, the addict's verbal attack will become the intervenors' best ammunition. As the group diffuses each argument by returning again and again to the basic facts, the addict will become exhausted, disarmed and ready to negotiate.

You can tell you've been successful as soon as the dependent calls for compromises. But that's when the group really bears down.

No Promises or Compromises

Don't hesitate to use any of the facts about the disease in this book. The addict has probably never heard them before. And the more you appear to know about what's happening to her, the more she will look at you with increased respect—if only realizing that you can't be spoon-fed any more bull. You'll have an advantage over her. Whether she wants to or not, she'll listen more intently to you.

Throw in things like, "Did you know . . ." It gets the dependent's attention focused on the disease, which most people know they can't control, and away from the charade.

You are after an unconditional surrender—not letting a shark off the hook because he promises to lie quietly in the net. All the promises he made to you in the past held more sludge than water. And each was followed by a series of half-attempts—like switching drugs or brands of booze or promising to cut down or never lose control again. The result was always far greater abuse.

The following responses have been cited by recovering alcoholics and drug addicts as the ones that they remember having the most effect in persuading them to get help.

Twenty Common Arguments and Responses

A. *It's my business and nobody else's. Ya hear?* (the John Wayne defense).

R. Well, it's our business now, because your drinking/using has affected all of us (the John Wayne offense). That's why we're here. Now we're going to tell you how it's affected us and what we are doing about it.

◆

A. *Other people are worse off than me.*

R. Do you really want to be as dumb as they are? You're the lucky one.

◆

A. *Maybe I don't want to get well.*

R. That's the disease talking, not you. The disease doesn't want you to get well and doesn't believe you can. We believe differently.

◆

A. *I can down more than any of you. I'll drink anyone under a table, and walk away. I can handle it.*

R. You only think you can. That's a sign that the addiction has already progressed and made chemical changes in your body. Next you'll suddenly lose all tolerance. But by then you may not be able to recover.

◆

A. *I don't drink/use that much anymore.*

R. You've lost your tolerance. That's a sign of the later stages of addiction.

◆

A. *My problem is only with hard stuff. (Vodka does it to me. I'm okay with wine.) I was thinking of switching anyway.*

R. No matter what the label—beer or scotch, mixed or not—they all have alcohol in them. You are allergic to alcohol, period. Alcohol is a Class A drug, and you are drug dependent.

R. (If other chemical) Your brain has changed. It is no longer relying on its own chemicals. It is all out of kilter, and any other mind-altering drug you use will make you a slave to a chemical.

◆

A. *I can think and work better with blow.*

R. You're mistaking motion for action. Sure, it gets your juices up, but it also fools you into thinking you're better than you are. You're going nowhere fast.

◆

A. *It helps me cope with the pain* (the loss of spouse, etc.).

R. Anesthetics can't remove pain; they just postpone it.

◆

A. *They* (the people or the pressures) *makes me use.*

R. "They" don't make you drink/use; *you* make you drink/use. There are plenty of people who have more problems than you'll ever have who don't drink/use.

◆

A. *The stuff only affects me when I use it. What I do on my time is my business.*

R. You're in withdrawal when you're not using. Your whole body is clamoring for more, and you can't possibly be keeping all your attention on what you're doing.

◆

A. *I know more about what's happening to me than you do. I can handle it myself. I just need a little more time. I know what's best for me.*

R. Your best thinking got you here. Do you really have any better thoughts? If you had some, why didn't you use them before now?

◆

A. *I'm not an addict. Look at me. I couldn't be a success if I were a drunk. (I'm not sleeping on vents on K Street.)*
R. So what? There's always someone worse than you, like the guy on the marble slab. Do you want to wait until you are there, too, so you can finally say, "There's nobody worse than me"?

◆

A. *Leave me alone—I'm happy where I am.* (The toughest but most common.)
R. Does it really make you happy to (cite examples: lose your wife or job, get in accidents, injure others, beat kids, go to jail, fall down stairs, etc.)? You don't have any problem so great that another bender won't make it even worse.

◆

A. *Okay, okay. I'll reform. I'll just drink socially* (or switch brands, use ice cubes, limit myself to two).
R. Social drinking is a contradiction in terms where you're concerned. When you drink, you get downright antisocial (present evidence). You're addicted to alcohol. It's not the quantity, quality or timing of the intake. You're a slave to a damned bottle.

◆

A. *What will people think? I can't afford to jeopardize my business reputation if people find out.*
R. What do you think people think of you now? Do you think no one notices when you're out cold standing up? Or don't you remember? (Give example.)

◆

A. *I'll lose my friends.*

R. The people who don't stick by you now were never your friends in the first place. Some will resent it because they can't control their own drinking/drugging. They aren't your real friends. They only care about you as long as you keep up the party. They don't care that it's killing you. They're just using you. The people that really care will admire you for your courage to change.

◆

A. *So what if I get drunk? I'm having fun. Life wouldn't be worth living without that. I'm willing to pay the price of a hangover.*

R. You can't see what you look like from the inside of your eyeballs. Falling into camp fires, losing car keys and jobs, making an ass out of yourself—people are either laughing at you or are very pissed off. Do you really count that as fun?

◆

A. *I'm not going to sit in a boring AA/NA meeting. Those people are losers. I'm going to control my drinking better.*

R. That's what AA people do. They are learning how to get back the power they lost. Sure, they were losers, just like you— addicted doctors, teachers, mechanics, accountants, sales- persons—with one big difference, they had the common sense to try something that has worked for millions of other people.

◆

A. *I can take care of it. I'm president of a damned company. I'll be okay. I don't need any help. I can do it myself. I'll just stop. Right now.*

R. I know you mean it, but most people can't. We feel it's best if you get help.

◆

A. *Thank you all, but I'm doing it myself.*

R. Okay. But if you can't stay straight and sober, then will you agree to get help?

The Bottom Line

The experience of a confrontation is like wrestling with a greased pig: the dependent will always try to get away. The one basic statement that seems to stop every counterattack dead in its tracks is: "Stop thinking. Your best thinking got you here."

How to Keep the Pressure On

◆

"Great golfers insist on winning. Winners are persistent and never give up because they know that the opponent's game can fall apart at any time. So they keep up the pressure by keeping their eye on the ball, and doing the next indicated thing. They keep their head down and play it as it lays, whether in the fairway or the rough. Never **give** up, never **give** in."
—Every good golfer

Just as in golf, follow-through determines the success of the intervention—how the club with the addiction message connects with the rather mealy brain of the dependent and follows through.

Require a response. Any let-up on your part will be immediately seized on as a sign of insincerity. Keep the pressure on after the intervention by carrying out all ultimatums. The dependent will never seek help if there is the slightest break in your swing.

Make sure that the people involved in the intervention will continue the follow-through with you. Keep in touch with one another. Become a mutual support system while addressing your collective chemical dependency problem (the dependent) until the problem is rehabilitated.

Ten of the Most Effective Recovery Ultimatums

Remember that the Recovery Ultimatum is your strongest ammunition. Use it to gain closure on the intervention and to enforce the terms. Here are 10 of the most convincing and effective we've encountered.

1. **Job:** "We value you here at the company. You've been a good friend as well as a good team player, and we want you to go even further with the company. You've got what it takes. But we can't afford to have you out of control. You get help now or you find another job."

2. **Divorce:** "I love you. I believe we can save our marriage and build a better one. But if you don't get help today, don't come home ever again. I have drawn up the papers for a divorce and a court order preventing you from ever seeing me again. Here they are. As soon as you take the next drink or drug, I'm signing them."

3. **Custody:** "The kids and I really care about you and want us to learn to love each other, to be a real family. But they're afraid and so am I. If you don't get help today, I'll seek a court order for custody of the kids."

4. **Inheritance:** "You mean too much to us to see this go on. We're all willing to do whatever it takes to help you in every way we can. But if you don't get help today, you're cut off. We have all agreed that no one is lending you any money or bailing you out again. Period."

5. **Lover:** "I love you, honey. You're everything I ever wanted in a man. I know that we can get it all back and be more than we ever were to each other. But I won't make love to a corpse. If you don't go with the guys right now and commit to quit with their help, I'm leaving you. My bags are packed. They're behind you. I'm not going to watch you die and see bits

of me destroyed in the process. You quit or I'm getting on with my life without you."

6. **Ownership:** "You helped build this company. It's got your blood and sweat in it. But it's got mine too and I'm not going to see you trash it all. I have papers here suing for control of the partnership and allowing me to sell your share and use the proceeds to cover your losses these last several months. You get help now or my attorney is getting these papers within the hour."

7. **Home:** "You are my flesh and blood, and this is your home. But unless you get help today and quit the drugs forever, you can never set foot in this house again."

8. **Police record:** "You get help today, right now, and your mom and I will do everything possible to get help for ourselves and make this a family we all want to be a part of. Otherwise, we're driving right over to the police station and turning this stuff in and you with it."

9. **Prison:** "I'm just an attorney, not a miracle worker. The judge says that he'll suspend sentence if you get into a treatment program today. Otherwise, it's six months, minimum, no bargaining."

10. **Reputation:** "You get help today and we've all agreed to come to treatment too for family therapy. Otherwise, I'm reporting this to the police. You may be president of the company, but you're going to be indicted on drug charges."

Use the ultimatum! It takes real guts, but it's worth the results. There is one condition: YOU MUST CARRY THROUGH WITH IT.

One woman gave her husband the ultimatum 40 times in 25 years. Despite his repeated broken promises, she never left him as she had threatened, and he went through treatment six times, with worse and worse relapses each time. The day she drew up the divorce papers and gave her attorney permission to file them if he learned that her husband was out drinking again, the guy finally committed to a recovery (although by then he needed a 90-day program to achieve it).

Ultimatums are fuel. If enforced, they will launch the recovery process. If not enforced, they will provide equal fuel to the disease and continual relapsing.

Never give an ultimatum unless you are prepared to carry it out fully and completely to the letter of the condition.

How Much to Tell

"People call it a 'terminological inexactitude.' God calls it a lie."

—Bishop Desmond Tutu

Never lie to someone during an intervention! It will be the pinhole that collapses the Grand Coulee Dam.

This is not to say that a little discretion isn't appropriate to avoid sending the dependent shrieking to the nearest toilet bowl.

You don't, for instance, tell the person that he is in for the roughest ride of his life; that many people, despite the best help, never do recover; that the disease will always be battling for her brain; that recovery will require more work than climbing out of quicksand.

You are not lying to the dependent. You are delaying some information that might work against getting her to the door of the recovery program.

(If God didn't manage to severely dull the brain of a woman during sex to forget the bone-cracking, muscle-racking, brain-scalding experience of her last childbirth, civilization would have come to an end a long time ago. Needless to say, no obstetric nurse reminds the woman of the impending pain as she happily trots in for her monthly physicals. After all, when the child is finally held and cuddled, the torture is forgotten. The reward is well worth the cost, whether it's the excruciating pain of giving birth or withdrawing from a chemical dependency.)

If you said it all, the goal of straightness and sobriety would seem utterly unachievable, leaving the dependent completely broken.

Almost everyone who quits using does it initially for the wrong reasons: They want to "get the heat off," and they fully intend to learn how to control their use—not give it up completely. So what? This half-compliance gives you the crack in the door to successful intervention.

No Volunteers, Just Victims

It has become fashionable in pop psychology to say that there are no victims, just volunteers. *But no one volunteers for addiction*—they had no idea what they were buying into with the first drink or drug. There were no crystal balls—a lot of horror stories but nothing bad happened in early and mid-stage drinking and using.

It's even truer that no one volunteers for recovery. Despite what they say, recovering addicts surrendered because they were forced to—mentally, physically, occupationally, socially, religiously, penally or conjugally. Make the surrender as easy as possible.

For example, what you don't reveal during the intervention is that the dependent:

1. Can never drink or use again.
2. Will probably need a spiritual program to have permanent recovery.
3. Will always be just one drink or drug away from total relapse.
4. Will have to change playgrounds and playmates.
5. Will have to give up everything about the old lifestyle.
6. Will never regain the ability to drink or use.

What you can let the dependent go on thinking, for now, is that:

1. Abstinence is not forever; just today.
2. Using isn't the problem, just a temporary solution.
3. Treatment or self-help will reveal how to control use.
4. The recovery is for the sake of others.

It is confidentiality that makes 12-step groups and treatment work. In fact, most first-timers sneak into their first group meeting with their collars up and their cars parked next door. Addicts are, above all else, paranoid, which means they think everyone is not only out to get them, but also checking up on them all the time. The truth is that everyone the addict knows knew about the abuse—nothing was hidden—and they will recognize a change and be relieved, including restaurant owners and bartenders, bosses and even buddies.

Questions About Recovery That You've Always Wanted to Ask, But . . .

◆

"I just hope that once Reggie recovers he'll get some of that romance back. . . . Why are you laughing?"

Families and friends of addicts in early recovery have many questions about issues like socializing, medications, relapse and sexuality. Here are the answers to those most often asked.

Can a dependent really regain mental and physical abilities in recovery?

In most cases, the brain and the body repair themselves if the dependency is arrested in time. Although some drugs can cause permanent damage, in general, recovering alcoholics and drug addicts—those who are abstinent and working a program of recovery—perform as well or better than their peers. The same can be said of anyone who is not handicapped by chemicals, maintains healthy behaviors and attitudes and focuses all his energies on living a life of responsibility and accountability. (For recovering addicts, this is essential. Any less would mean relapse or death.) There are several other explanations for the increased performance. For example, a majority of addicts were workaholic and overachievers before their addictions. In recovery they returned to work with the same commitment and dedication, but with tools to help them prevent burnout. Moreover, since the percentage of addicts found among achievers and intellectually gifted people is greater than the general population, it follows that these people would excel in recovery. But each person's recovery is an individual situation depending equally on attitude and physical condition.

How will sobriety affect our sex life?

The so-called "aphrodisiac effect" associated with alcohol, narcotics and depressants is really a depressing of the central nervous system. It not only lowers inhibitions, but the ability to sustain a physical response. Impotency and frigidity are very common in addiction—especially where the addictive chemicals block off the ability of sex hormones to work on the brain. As Shakespeare said, it "provokes the desire, but takes away the performance. . . . "

Early in recovery, most people experience a new level of openness and honesty, a reawakening of their sexual drive and a heightened desire. But for many, the concept of sex without "loosening up" is terrifying—like "the first time" all over again. Some people are so overwhelmed by the surfacing of feelings that had long been medicated and repressed—anger, pain, fear, loss—they find they must address these first before they are comfortable with intimacy. Similarly, spouses who have not begun their own recovery program may find themselves in the middle of the "numbies," in the depression stage of the healing process, and unable to respond.

Because sexual reactions are an individual issue, a family program and aftercare involving both partners together is critical. When partners are seeking help together, a new openness, honesty, compassion, willingness and love can grow, making for a healthy and mutually rewarding sex life. Getting there requires patience and sensitivity on both parts. The most important thing to remember is that intimacy in any form, like everything else in recovery, is a part of a program of living that demands responsibility, honesty and morality.

Will he/she be able to go to parties without feeling the compulsion to drink?

Initially, every recovering person is frightened of the first trip to a grocery store displaying wine or beer, the first visit to a restaurant, the first plane flight or sporting event, and especially the first social gathering with drinking or using friends. Each person's recovery is an individual thing. But recovering people will always be faced with situations where drinking or using is extremely easy. It is best to be honest about these situations. If the recovering person is struggling with the craving, then avoid "slippery places." In later recovery, most people can easily attend functions where liquor is served and enjoy their soda, fruit drink or coffee without discomfort.

What should I say if someone asks me what my husband wants to drink?

Ask your husband what he wants you to say. The easiest response is, "Let me ask him" or "Why don't you ask him and see?" If he is elsewhere and an associate offers to bring or order an alcoholic drink for him, some recovering people ask their spouses to explain, "He can't drink—doctor's orders," "He'd like the hard stuff, but then we really wouldn't like him, so how about a soft drink?" or "He's allergic to alcohol, but he'll have a tonic if you have some around." Others prefer it straight up: "John wants you to know he is a recovering alcoholic. He'd love a cup of black coffee."

Can I keep wine around the house?

That is between you and your spouse or roommate. Again, if it's a problem in early sobriety to be around the alcohol, it's best for everyone not to have it around.

What about all the drinking buddies?

If your dependent's close friends all require alcohol or other drugs to socialize with each other, he or she may soon find they have little in common after all. Once the recovering person starts avoiding slippery places (bars, casinos, hotel lobby happy hours, keggers, etc.), some of the "old friends" will begin to fade away. Most recovering people find themselves with the solid old friends who enjoy them for who they really are and don't need the alcohol or drugs around. Others prefer to seek out new playgrounds and new playmates—people who enjoy the same degree of openness, honesty, humor and conversation, and for whom drugs are not a part of the picture.

What will I serve when we entertain?

That's a common question. The recovering person should decide how he or she feels about others drinking. If it is not a problem, it is always easiest to suggest that the guests bring whatever they would like to drink. Otherwise, decide mutually what you will tell the guests ("Joe asks that we not serve alcohol, at least for a few weeks").

Will he/she see me differently?

Whether or not you realize it, you both have been changing mentally and emotionally as you have grown older. Although some of these changes may have been camouflaged by the dependency, they will become apparent in recovery, especially as a new openness and honesty enter the relationship. You may find that in many ways you are starting your relationship all over. It can be an adventurous, exciting and rewarding discovery. The most important thing is that you be friends to one another and let the relationship take its course. As they say in AA, "Acceptance is the answer to all my problems today."

What kind of emotional changes can I expect in my partner?

That is difficult to predict. The addiction psychosis (depression, mood swings, anger, paranoia, resentments, isolation, memory losses, skittishness, etc.) will disappear early on. But without a narcotic to numb memories, many other hidden feelings may surface. The emotional healing process is normal—a recovering addict experiences denial, fear-anger, manipulation, depression and eventually acceptance of his disease, in that sequence, just as if he or she lost an arm or a spouse. Part of the rocky road to recovery is learning to accept and deal constructively with these feelings without an outside chemical coper. Out-patient counseling and aftercare groups can speed up the emotional recovery process.

What kind of emotional changes can I expect in me?

Almost the same ones as your partner, with a few more thrown in—frustration, separation, abandonment, confusion, helplessness, guilt, vengeance and jealousy. Obviously, you will need the help of others who are experiencing the same things to understand that you are not losing your mind but regaining it. A program of recovery is critical to move beyond the destructive feelings toward those of acceptance, gratitude, self-respect, serenity and unconditional love. Look into Al-Anon or another self-help support program for families and close friends.

My partner has a 37-year-old body and a 16-year-old brain. Will he ever grow up?

Once a person relies on mood-altering chemicals, his emotional maturation stops. If he was 18 when he began abusing, he will have the emotional maturity of an 18-year-old when he begins recovery. But with continued abstinence, therapy and a program of living, the maturation process will continue where it left off—the time frame is determined by the quality of the sobriety.

Will I get over my anger?

That depends on you. Emotions are neither good nor bad—they simply ARE. It is what we do with them that is good or bad—for ourselves and others. The anger is constructive if it is discussed openly and objectively and used to bring about a change that helps both parties.

Will prescription painkillers cause a relapse?

They present several problems: (1) They dull the senses enough that the recovering person may lose the fear of relapse and drink or use the chemical of choice again. (2) Every person, once addicted, is predisposed to develop a dependency to any other mind-altering chemical. The recovering person should be honest with physicians, nurses and dentists about his condition, use prescription painkillers only when absolutely necessary for pain, follow the exact dose on the label and avoid refilling the prescription.

What about cough medicines and mouthwashes?

Relapses have occurred as a result of using cough medicines or mouthwashes that contain alcohol. The person starts out swallowing a little, then increases the frequency without realizing that the craving has returned. It is best to avoid them.

Should someone keep an eye on him/her?

No. There aren't enough eyes in the entire universe if the dependent decides to drink or use again. The best policy is to go about your business. If behavior is strange, confront it. If you stumble across evidence of a relapse, confront the person. Discuss it in aftercare or with a counselor. Keep your eyes open but focus your attention on your own recovery.

What are the signs of a relapse?
Usually there are several:

1. Discontinuing work on a program of recovery, with the excuse, "I'm doing great without it."
2. A failure to attend self-help groups or aftercare, with the excuse, "I'd rather do it on my own."
3. Criticism of other recovering people, with the excuse, "They're a bunch of losers."
4. A return to old playgrounds and playmates with the excuse, "I'm just having some innocent fun."
5. Experimentation with other chemicals than the drug of choice, with the excuse, "I never had a problem with this."
6. Experimentation with the chemical of choice, with the excuse, "See, I can control it."
7. Denial of an addiction, with the excuse, "I've been drinking or using again and nothing bad has happened this time. I wasn't really an addict."
8. Out-of-control drinking or using, with the excuse, "It's my life. I'm doing this because I want to, not because I have to."

What is "pink clouding"?

As the brain clears, health returns and the body again produces its own natural uppers, people experience a euphoric "pink cloud" where everything looks rosy. The sensation, which feels much like falling in love, doesn't last forever, and the body soon comes down and reestablishes a homeostasis. But the return to normal can be depressing to the person who seeks a permanent high. It is best to remember that, in feelings and physics, what goes up must come down.

How can I help avoid relapse?

Call it as you see it. Don't nag or play Mother or Big Brother. Share your honest feelings, point out the problem and, as much as possible, detach. Go about your business. Get to a counselor or an Al-Anon meeting. Bring it up in aftercare and discuss your concerns. Where relapse seems inevitable, Recovery Ultimatums can be very effective but only if they are delivered clearly, responsibly and unemotionally and are fully carried out.

How intimate do people become in treatment?

They learn a lot about each other. Many spouses worry about the close living situation. But men and women live in separate patient residences. Treatment is hard business, and everyone is focused on surviving. An awareness of one's self and one's appearance is typical in the second or third week of recovery, as well as an awareness of others. Counselors keep a close eye on patient behavior. Innocent flirtations may release pressure, but anything more can sabotage recovery for both parties and is strictly prohibited.

As an employer, how can I support recovery?

In many ways.

1. Recognize and compliment the recovering person for his or her incredible accomplishment. (It may not seem like much to you, but overcoming an addiction is the biggest thing the person has ever done in his or her life!)

2. Treat the recovering employee exactly like any other employee recovering from a temporary physical disability.

3. Respect his or her anonymity.

4. Have an employment policy that encourages admitting problems and seeking help rather than penalizing people for their disabilities or their honesty.

5. Provide adequate employee benefits in the form of insurance coverage for treatment and aftercare and a flexible leave policy for those seeking outside help for a chemical dependency problem.

6. Establish a drug-free workplace by publishing and upholding a policy that firmly opposes the use of alcohol or drugs in the workplace and lays out the terms for violation, as well as the conditions for performance review and referral.

7. Encourage employees to participate in self-help groups and, if they desire, to hold meetings on the premises.

8. Recognize the negative impact of alcohol on performance and discourage its use at company functions.

9. Hire an employee assistance consultant as an objective and confidential third party to work with labor and management and to help employees with performance, dependency or adjustment difficulties.

10. Keep an open heart, an open mind and an open eye. Do not hesitate to document and confront performance problems or refer for assessment if you suspect a problem or the danger of a relapse—the earlier the better! Don't enable slips by allowing or excusing them. Be supportive but firm.

Enjoying the Rewards

◆

"The quality of mercy is not strained. . . . It is twice blest.
It blesseth him that gives, and him that receives."
—William Shakespeare, *The Merchant of Venice*

What are the rewards for all your time, effort, anxiety and care? Sometimes they aren't easy to see—especially at first. You can't expect any hugs and kisses right away, or even a "thank you." The people most affected by the dependency—the victim, family and close friends—will be so absorbed in the sheer blood, sweat and tears of early recovery that you may be the last thought on their minds (if you're lucky!).

Don't congratulate yourself on your success. Nobody gets anyone else clean and sober except the dependent and his Higher Power. It's often said that "the devil never tempts us with such success as when we view with satisfaction the fruits of our own labors.''

Counselors, interventionists, the recovering and their families have learned that no matter how much you care about the person who still suffers, you can't control recovery any more than the first drink.

Believing you have power you don't have sets you up for the guilt, resentment and blame that follows if the person cannot stay clean and sober. Realistically, there may be some slips and hiccups. Recovery is a process. Just because you dared to confront doesn't mean you ran the 500-meter relay and crossed the finish line yourself! You haven't achieved any more than monkey-wrenching the using, hopefully forever. But that's not up to you.

You can't expect to see results right away. Sobriety is a process—not an end—involving many phases beyond quitting: first hand-wringing abstinence; then reality facing—learning how to function in the world as if he couldn't drink milk while feeling like he lost a leg; and finally full performance. It's a long and winding road spattered with potholes and pitfalls.

There is a reward for your trouble. It's the hardest thing to communicate without having the experience yourself. Only those who have experienced it know that it transcends every other human achievement. All else pales beside it.

It's not something you can spend, eat, drive or even brag about. But it's yours alone. Call it an emotion if you want, because the indescribable reward is a feeling first. But, unlike most, it lasts your whole lifetime. The key word is "life." You reached out to help save a life. This must be mankind's first call because the feeling dwarfs that of every other accomplishment you've ever had. This is a promise and a guarantee. Try it. It will spoil materialism forever.

Why Bad Things Happen

Sometimes we don't see much progress, especially when we watch the struggle a recovering addict is having (and may always have). It's hard to accept any possible justification for the devastation of addiction.

Most dependents *never* find help. They die of their addiction and take tens of thousands of innocent people with them.

We know the consuming hatred, paranoia and ego-obsessive aggression of addiction psychosis. We wonder what life would have been like if the fate of the world weren't so often in the hands of brilliant and charismatic strategists who were also hopeless, mindless addicts, like Alexander, Napoleon and Hitler. We may never understand why bad things are allowed to exist, but we all have moral choices to make.

The mystery is that when bad things happen, many good and innocent people are hurt. The miracle is that great disasters can lead to greater victories.

Like the often painful legacy of history, addiction can become more than a rotting mountain of manure but, rather, fertile ground for a better future.

In the Bible, Paul best summarizes this hope: "Through love, God turns all things to their good." Love has to be the main motivation in any attempt to help an addict because we can give it unconditionally. (Otherwise, it's just bargaining, not love.)

We have a prayer hanging in our home that says, "We don't know what pleases you, God. But we know that trying to please you does." The one thing that surely pleases your God is saving a life and ending the senseless destruction to countless others. Each person maimed by addiction is His child.

The Mission and the Miracle

Your Mission Impossible, if you choose to accept it, is to convince someone that he or she may, after sweaty nights that won't end and days empty of pleasure, become happy, joyous and free WHEN HE OR SHE THINKS THEY ALREADY ARE and this is the best they can hope for. That's your competition.

And yet the miracle of "clean and sober" happens with regularity. Why? It is beyond the power of any who have experienced or witnessed it to fully explain what has happened. It just does, in spite of people who die, marriages that break up and jobs that are lost, even in sobriety. It happens—in spite of the moral, financial, physical and spiritual bankruptcy that newly recovering people must face straight and sober—unprotected by the thick, armor-plated slavery of an altered mind. In the cold light of day where the world suddenly has sharp edges, it happens.

Sometimes it really is a white-light, burning-bush experience—as it was for Bill W., founder of AA. But usually early sobriety is a trudge along the muddy "road to happy destiny" that most AA's speak of. Only after a while does the recovering person realize that the unbelievable, a miracle, has happened.

There was a last drink, snort, pill or needle, and then no more—even though their whole being centered around those things just the day before!

Why? The closest anyone has come to answer that is because someone—you—at last tried to help, whether greatly or poorly seems to make small difference. The fact that someone tried may be all it takes. Someone at last has shown they care for, not despise, the sufferer—care, in fact, more than the victim cares for himself or herself. Maybe it's curiosity: "What do they see in me that I can't see?" Maybe it's because deep down most addicts know something is very wrong.

Whenever they try to put a finger on it, the other four join in a conditioned reflex around the glass, pill, straw or needle.

Maybe that's why AA works in spite of the insurmountable obstacles. Its cornerstone is to help the alcoholic who still suffers *while* (not after) the helper is still suffering himself.

Psychologically this makes sense, because it takes one's mind off one's own troubles. Moreover, two people are helped, not just one. Could it have some connection with "When two or more gather in My name . . ."? Could it be that it can't be explained by any reasonable or rational philosophy of this world?

Recovering people know that you can't see electricity either, but when you see the results, you can no longer deny that it exists and come to believe with all your soul that it does.

Best wishes, and God bless you!

Appendices

◆

A

Detachment:
The First Step to a
Loved One's Recovery

◆

By picking up the pieces, coping and trying to help, people innocently "enable" a loved one's addiction to worsen by postponing the consequences. They become co-dependent. Recovery for all requires learning new behaviors, the most important of which is detachment.

Detachment means to stop enabling and to do what we are supposed to do without taking over the responsibilities and problems of the addict. It means being emotionally objective while continuing to live, let live and love.

Detachment IS NOT denial. Some people won't discuss the alcohol or drug problem of a loved one. They think this is detachment, but it is denial. The problem will only get worse as long as it is hidden. To detach, we acknowledge the problem openly and deny instead the compelling instinct to lie, excuse, hide or avoid the subject. We admit that someone we care about has an alcohol or drug problem and that we cannot cure or fix it no matter how much we care. Detachment IS admitting the dependency.

Detachment DOES NOT MEAN to avoid confronting. Arguing with the addict is fruitless and destructive, but some people think that detachment means to avoid an intervention. Or they mistake people-pleasing and peacemaking, which are forms of enabling, for detachment. This is like tip-toeing over live grenades instead of doing what is necessary to remove them. Detachment requires being honest and open, recognizing the problems, refusing to argue and carrying through with all ultimatums. Detachment during an intervention allows an open communication of facts and feelings, a respect for self and others and an acceptance of (not necessarily agreement with) each other's choices while taking care of oneself. Detachment IS confronting problems.

Detachment DOES NOT replace personal responsibility. To detach, we must allow dependents to face the full consequences of their actions by not taking on their unfulfilled responsibilities. Yet detachment cannot occur unless we fully perform our own responsibilities as spouses, family, friends and members of society—otherwise we are no better than the addict. As citizens, we share an obligation to uphold the law. This includes reporting drunk driving. Co-dependents are not absolved from being responsible members of the human race. Detachment IS performing our duties.

Detachment IS NOT isolating yourself from others. Some people think that detachment means minding one's own business and letting addicts "live and let live," even when they are hurting others. Where abused children, battered spouses, young addicts or the mentally ill are concerned, minding our own business is akin to benign murder—standing by while people drown who have no ability to swim. We must help the victims to get help, take care of ourselves and let go of the outcomes. Detachment IS human responsibility.

Detachment DOES NOT replace feeling. Detachment removes our anger and obsession. But some people use it as an excuse for frigidity, desertion, rejection or other ways to punish the dependent. To detach, we accept what we cannot change— the dependent. And we change what we can—our co-dependent behaviors. We do this by refusing to deny, enable or be victimized, seeking outside help, confronting and keeping all ultimatums. By detaching, we accept and care about the dependent without accepting or caring for his behavior. Our feelings are no longer determined by the addict's behavior. Thus: detachment IS unconditional love.

B

Emotions and Feelings Checklist: An Alcohol and Drug Intervention Tool

◆

The more honestly, openly and calmly you can share what you feel about the dependent and the chemical abuse, the more effective the intervention will be. Identify the most common feelings and prepare to talk about them during the intervention. Begin with the words, "As a result of (your actions), I feel . . ."

Unpleasant Feelings

Abandoned	Consumed	Disgusted
Abused	Controlling	Drained
Alienated	Deadened	Doomed
Angry	Deceived	Dumped on
Anxious	Deceptive	Embarrassed
Argumentative	Defiant	Empty
Blaming	Denying	Enraged
Brain-washed	Depressed	Estranged
Bullied	Desperate	Exhausted
Compromised	Despondent	Failed
Confused	Determined	Fearful

Foolish	Judgmental	Resentful
Forgotten	Justified	Restless
Frenzied	Lonely	Sad
Friendless	Lost	Scared
Frightened	Lustful	Self-righteous
Frigid	Manipulated	Self-surviving
Frustrated	Manipulative	Shy
Futile	Martyred	Scattered
Guilty	Materialistic	Superior
Harmful	Miserable	Tenuous
Helpless	Misjudged	Tested
Hopeless	Mistrusted	Trapped
Hostile	Nauseated	Traumatized
Humiliated	Numb	Unfaithful
Hurt	Out-of-control	Used
Impatient	Pissed	Wasted
Impotent	Pitied	Workaholic
Inadequate	Pitiful	Worried
Inhibited	Pity	Vindictive
Insecure	Powerless	Violent
Intimidated	Reactive	Vulnerable
Isolated	Rebellious	Zapped
Jealous	Rejected	

Sometimes the most difficult part of sharing honest feelings in a CARE intervention is during the second step when you "Affirm" the worth of the dependent and convey your desire to see the person recover. The weight of the unpleasant emotions may block the love and care you really may feel. But it is these positive affirmations that convey hope and can inspire the dependent to commit fully to recovery. Review the following list of pleasant feelings. Pick the two or three most appropriate. Practice by beginning with the words, "Despite all of this, I really feel/am _____. I want to see you recover." This is only an example. Use your own words. Practice describing the good feeling to him/her and explaining it.

Pleasant/Supportive Feelings

Admiring	Loving
Caring	Loyal
Concerned	Protective
Dedicated	Ready
Faithful	Responsible
Forgiving	Sorry
Friendly	Supportive
Hopeful	Sympathetic
Humanitarian	Understanding
Inspired	Willing

If you can't say anything positive, don't be afraid to at least say, "Somewhere inside I know I must really care about you because. . . . [give reason]. But I've been through so much I can't feel it right now."

C

Listing the Objective Facts: An Alcohol and Drug Intervention Tool

◆

Before the intervention, it is best for all participants to recall the facts concerning the dependent's behavior. This will not only help refresh memories but also can reveal the extent of the dependency, reassure you, and arm you with the facts you'll need for the intervention. List the approximate date of the most recent incident; state what happened; state what you did as a result; and state how you felt. Do the same for the next to the last incident and so on. (Some examples are: fight, DUI, accident, mistake, work-related problem, blackout [memory loss], embarrassing others, losing car, losing paycheck, credit problems, lies, etc.) Discuss your notes with other participants and compare observations.

Date	What Happened	What You Did	How You Felt
___	_____	_____	_____
___	_____	_____	_____
___	_____	_____	_____
___	_____	_____	_____

Date	What Happened	What You Did	How You Felt
____	_____	_____	_____
____	_____	_____	_____
____	_____	_____	_____
____	_____	_____	_____
____	_____	_____	_____
____	_____	_____	_____
____	_____	_____	_____
____	_____	_____	_____
____	_____	_____	_____
____	_____	_____	_____

Source: P. J. Mahoney, C.E.A.P., interventionist

D

Are You Co-dependent?

♦

Once a person begins the downward cycle to addiction, those closest to him (family, friends and even co-workers) begin compensating to try to reestablish balance. Without knowing it, they develop behavior patterns which allow the dependency to continue. Eventually, they become emotionally and even physically ill. The following is a list of typical questions posed by addictions therapists and organizations established to help the dependent's family and friends.

Is there a chemically dependent person in your life?

YES NO

☐ ☐ 1. Has this person's drinking or using ever caused you embarrassment?

☐ ☐ 2. Does this person's drinking or using make the atmosphere uncomfortable and tense?

☐ ☐ 3. Has this person ever had a loss of memory as a result of drinking or using?

☐ ☐ 4. Are you concerned about this person's association with other heavy drinkers or drug users?

YES NO

☐ ☐ 5. Has this person made and broken numerous promises to stop drinking or using?

☐ ☐ 6. Does this person expect you to lie and make excuses to cover up his/her drinking or using?

☐ ☐ 7. Has this person's use of alcohol or drugs caused difficulty on the job, at home or socially?

☐ ☐ 8. Has this person's drinking or using ever caused a medical, legal or financial problem?

☐ ☐ 9. Is the person's drinking or using affecting his or her reputation?

☐ ☐ 10. Has anyone outside the family ever expressed concern about this person's use of alcohol or drugs?

☐ ☐ 11. Does this person consider holidays, weekends and special events as drinking or drugging celebrations?

☐ ☐ 12. Does this person use drinks or drugs in response to good news and bad news?

☐ ☐ 13. Do you or others get upset or uneasy whenever this person is present?

☐ ☐ 14. Does this person refuse to allow discussion of his/her drinking or using?

☐ ☐ 15. Do you feel that, if pushed, this person would choose the chemical over continuing your relationship?

☐ ☐ 16. When under the influence of alcohol or drugs, does this person drive a car?

YES NO

☐ ☐ 17. Does this person drink or use to build self-confidence?

☐ ☐ 18. Does this person often try to rationalize or explain away the need for alcohol or drugs?

☐ ☐ 19. Does this person keep a ready supply of alcohol or drugs hidden away from others in peculiar places?

☐ ☐ 20. Does this person regularly frequent places where alcohol or drugs are heavily used?

Note: Yes to five or more may indicate a dependency problem. Seek out a professional for an accurate assessment.

Are you co-dependent?

YES NO

☐ ☐ 1. Do you often find yourself trying to control someone else's drinking or using?

☐ ☐ 2. Do most of your thoughts center on the chemically dependent person or the problems he/she causes?

☐ ☐ 3. Do you find yourself denying the problem and/or finding excuses for the person's chemical abuse?

☐ ☐ 4. Do you try to cover up the person's drinking or using or lie on his/her behalf?

☐ ☐ 5. Do you feel somehow responsible for the person's chemical abuse?

☐ ☐ 6. Do you feel guilty when the chemically dependent abuses you or others—physically or verbally?

YES NO

☐   ☐   7. Do you avoid attending family or social events with the chemically dependent?

☐   ☐   8. Do you often find yourself unable to sleep because of the chemically dependent person?

☐   ☐   9. Do you often make threats about the person's chemical use and fail to follow through on them?

☐   ☐   10. Do you often fantasize about the chemically dependent's permanent disappearance, or your own?

☐   ☐   11. Do you extract promises from the dependent about the chemical use even though they are never kept?

☐   ☐   12. Have you withdrawn from outside activities and friendships because of shame over the dependency?

☐   ☐   13. Do you or your children ride with the chemically influenced driver even though you are afraid?

☐   ☐   14. Do you have the sense of walking on robin's eggs when you are around the chemically dependent?

☐   ☐   15. Do you find yourself "editing" everything you will say before you speak to the dependent?

☐   ☐   16. Do you stay in the presence of the chemically dependent even when you feel physically threatened?

☐   ☐   17. Do you avoid issuing an ultimatum because you fear being alone or losing the relationship?

YES NO

☐ ☐ 18. Do you often take the role of the practical and strong "survivor" whose major problem is the dependent?

☐ ☐ 19. Do you find your moods swing as a direct result of the dependent's moods and behaviors?

☐ ☐ 20. Do you hide, dilute, substitute, or search and destroy the dependent's alcohol or drugs?

☐ ☐ 21. Do you feel less and less happy with yourself, or more and more critical of others?

☐ ☐ 22. Do you find you've taken over many of the chemically dependent's duties and responsibilities?

☐ ☐ 23. Do you feel forced to increase your control over the family's expenditures, despite less and less success?

☐ ☐ 24. Do you often bail the chemically dependent person out of financial or legal problems?

☐ ☐ 25. Do you try to make the children accept the dependent's behavior despite their withdrawal or rebellion?

☐ ☐ 26. Where this applies, do you use sex to manipulate or refuse sex to punish the chemically dependent?

☐ ☐ 27. Similarly, do you lie, fake it or make excuses when "turned off" sexually to the chemically dependent?

☐ ☐ 28. Do you suffer from nervous reactions (nausea, stomach knots, ulcers, twitching, bitten fingernails)?

YES NO

☐ ☐ 29. Do you tend to complain about the dependent and seek out the sympathy of others?

☐ ☐ 30. Do you find you must rely on alcohol or prescription drugs, food, work or an affair in order to cope?

Note: Yes to seven or more may indicate a co-dependency. Seek out a professional for an accurate assessment.

References: Al-Anon, the Johnson Institute, Hazelden Educational Foundation, Life Center at Sun Valley, Serenity Lane of Eugene.

E

Are You Alcoholic?

◆

Often the person with the alcohol problem is among the last to recognize it. The line between social drinking and pathological drinking is almost invisible. To learn whether you may have crossed over it, ask yourself these questions. They represent the typical questions posed by addictions therapists and organizations established to help the alcoholic. Alcoholism is a chronic, progressive and fatal illness that can be arrested and successfully treated.

YES NO

☑ ☐ 1. Do you often fail to keep promises to yourself about cutting out, cutting down or controlling your drinking?

☐ ☐ 2. Do you prefer to drink alone (even though it "looks better" if you don't)?

☑ ☐ 3. Do you attend events on the basis of whether alcohol will be served?

☐ ☐ 4. Do you ever need an "eye-opener" the next morning?

YES NO

☑ ☐ 5. Are you more anxious to get your first drink than you used to be?

☑ ☐ 6. Do you keep close track of the quantity and location of your available booze?

☐ ☐ 7. Do you find you need to drink more and more booze to achieve the same effect?

☑ ☐ 8. Have you ever forgotten what happened while or after drinking even though you didn't pass out (black out)?

☑ ☐ 9. Do you ever sneak drinks before, during or after drinking with others?

☑ ☐ 10. Do you experience frequent, unpredictable mood swings (highs and lows)?

☑ ☐ 11. Do you find it hard to concentrate during or after drinking?

☑ ☐ 12. Have you lost your ambition, persistence or competitive edge?

☑ ☐ 13. Does your family comment about your drinking?

☐ ☐ 14. Do you tremble inside unless you continue drinking?

☐ ☐ 15. Do you wake up in the night with the shakes, unable to return to sleep?

☑ ☐ 16. Do you find yourself often jumpy, restless, irritable and likely to fly off the handle?

☑ ☐ 17. Do people or circumstances "make you drink"?

YES NO

☑ ☐ 18. Do you often feel afraid without reason and seek out a drink to conquer the fear?

☑ ☐ 19. Does it annoy you when others drink too slowly or leave drinks unfinished?

☑ ☐ 20. During or after drinking, have you said or done things you wished you hadn't?

☑ ☐ 21. Do you find yourself craving a drink at a certain time of day?

☑ ☐ 22. Does drinking cause you physical problems or complaints?

☑ ☐ 23. Do others comment on your drinking or try to limit it?

☐ ☐ 24. Are you less and less selective about your drinking companions and environments?

☑ ☐ 25. Have your resentments, jealousies and dislikes increased since drinking?

☐ ☐ 26. Has your drinking ever caused a problem in your job or your business?

☑ ☐ 27. Do you find it difficult to turn down a drink?

☐ ☐ 28. Are you losing your sex drive?

☐ ☐ 29. Can you stop drinking when someone tells you to for as long as they specify?

☑ ☐ 30. Do you get angry when people make comments about your drinking?

☐ ☐ 31. Do you hide your liquor?

YES NO

☐ ☐ 32. When you drink, do you often end up drunk?

☐ ☐ 33. Is getting drunk ever the object of your drinking?

☑ ☐ 34. Do you forget to eat when you're drinking?

☑ ☐ 35. Lately, do you get drunk sooner than you expect?

☐ ☐ 36. Do you ever hallucinate?

☑ ☐ 37. Do you suffer increasing periods of depression and stay depressed longer?

☐ ☐ 38. Has drinking ever preceded an incident where you needed medical attention or were hospitalized?

☑ ☐ 39. Are you one of the last to leave a party where liquor is served?

☑ ☐ 40. Do "problems" cause you to drink?

☑ ☐ 41. Do you promise yourself to cut down when "things" get better?

☑ ☐ 42. Are you ever afraid of running out of booze?

☑ ☐ 43. Do you often drink to steady your nerves?

☑ ☐ 44. Do you find you need a drink to perform better?

☑ ☐ 45. Have you said to yourself or others, "I can quit any time I want; I just haven't really wanted to"?

☑ ☐ 46. Do you ever feel guilty or remorseful about your drinking?

☑ ☐ 47. Do you use excuses for your drinking (to celebrate, to cope, because you're happy, because you're sad)?

YES NO

☐ ☐ 48. Do you often like "a stiff one" after a polite sociable drinking occasion?

☑ ☐ 49. Do you increasingly feel that others are watching you or are "out to get you"?

☑ ☐ 50. Do you ever try to deceive others about your drinking?

Note: Yes to 10 or more may indicate a dependency. Seek a professional for an accurate assessment.

References: Alcoholics Anonymous, the Johnson Institute, Hazelden Educational Foundation, Life Center at Sun Valley, Serenity Lane of Eugene.

F

Are You Drug Addicted?

◆

The person with an addiction to a chemical substance, whether to an over-the-counter or prescription medication, a commercial product (like certain inhalants) or an illegal drug, is often the last to know. The line between use and dependency is invisible. To discover whether you may have crossed it, ask yourself these questions. They are typical of the questions posed by addictions therapists and organizations established to help the chemically dependent. Drug addiction is a chronic, progressive and fatal illness that can be arrested and successfully treated.

YES NO

☐ ☐ 1. Do you often break promises to yourself about cutting out, cutting down or controlling your drug use?

☐ ☐ 2. Have you ever lied to a doctor to get prescription drugs or used several doctors to get extra drugs?

☐ ☐ 3. Have you ever stolen drugs or stolen money or goods to buy drugs?

☐ ☐ 4. Do threats from others fail to stop you from using?

YES NO

☐ ☐   5. Do you lie, create alibis or otherwise make excuses for using?

☐ ☐   6. Does paying for your drug(s) of choice take precedence over your other financial responsibilities?

☐ ☐   7. Is it difficult to stop using if someone else tells you to?

☐ ☐   8. Has your drug use ever caused you legal, financial, job or family problems?

☐ ☐   9. Are you afraid of running out?

☐ ☐ 10. Do you try to keep a supply hidden in several unusual places?

☐ ☐ 11. Do you feel it's impossible to live without your drug(s) of choice?

☐ ☐ 12. Do you often question your sanity?

☐ ☐ 13. Would you rather use "recreational drugs" alone?

☐ ☐ 14. Do you ever wish you were dead?

☐ ☐ 15. Are you ever defensive, remorseful, guilty or ashamed about your drug use?

☐ ☐ 16. Are the drugs almost always foremost on your mind?

☐ ☐ 17. Do you have irrational, undefinable fears?

☐ ☐ 18. Have you ever used a mind-altering substance you didn't like because it was the only thing around?

YES NO

☐ ☐ 19. Do you keep using even when it causes serious problems?

☐ ☐ 20. Do you think you may have a drug problem?

☐ ☐ 21. Do you often use up your supply sooner than you expected?

☐ ☐ 22. Do you ever choose your friends and activities according to the alcohol or drugs available?

☐ ☐ 23. Is cost of the drugs the only thing stopping you from using more?

☐ ☐ 24. Since using, are you losing your sex drive?

☐ ☐ 25. Are you often the last to leave a place where alcohol or drugs are served?

☐ ☐ 26. Do you get high sooner or later than you used to or want to?

☐ ☐ 27. Has your sense of morality and ethics gone downhill since using?

☐ ☐ 28. Do you ever sell to others to help pay for your drugs?

☐ ☐ 29. Are you constantly afraid that others will notice your drug use?

☐ ☐ 30. Have you stopped caring about your behavior or appearance in public?

☐ ☐ 31. Is it hard to turn down drugs offered to you?

☐ ☐ 32. Are you afraid that if you stop using your drug, your work would suffer?

YES NO

☐ ☐ 33. Does thinking about using distract you?

☐ ☐ 34. Is using not as much fun as it used to be?

☐ ☐ 35. Do you sometimes wish someone or something would stop you?

☐ ☐ 36. Do you "load up" frantically and find yourself unable to control the quantity you take?

☐ ☐ 37. Do you ever sneak your drug of choice?

☐ ☐ 38. Are you less selective about your companions?

☐ ☐ 39. Are you more careless about your responsibilities and the welfare of close ones?

☐ ☐ 40. Have you lost your ambition?

☐ ☐ 41. Have your resentments, jealousies and dislikes increased?

☐ ☐ 42. Must you take drugs to have a good time?

☐ ☐ 43. Have you recently thought about suicide?

☐ ☐ 44. Do you often feel lost and abandoned?

☐ ☐ 45. Do you sometimes find that no one else makes any sense?

☐ ☐ 46. Do you get into fights over your drugs (quantity, availability, sharing)?

☐ ☐ 47. Will you use anything you don't like just to get high?

☐ ☐ 48. Is getting stoned the main object of your using?

YES   NO

☐   ☐   49. Do you crave your drug at a specific time of day?

☐   ☐   50. Since using, have you had any three of these symptoms: jittery, depressed, irritable, paranoid, distracted, lost memory, hallucinating, repetitious (combing hair, etc.), breathing problems, nausea, seizures or convulsions?

Note: Yes to 10 or more may indicate a dependency. Seek a professional for an accurate assessment.

References: Narcotics Anonymous, the Johnson Institute, Hazelden Educational Foundation, Life Center at Sun Valley, Serenity Lane of Eugene.

Bibliography

◆

Adult Children of Alcoholics. Janet Woititz. Health Communications, 1986.

Alcoholics Anonymous. AA World Services, 1955, 1986.

The Alcoholics Anonymous Experience. M. A. Maxwell. McGraw-Hill, 1984.

Am I an Addict? Narcotics Anonymous. World Services Office, 1986.

Another Chance: Hope and Health for the Alcoholic Family. Sharon Wegscheider. Science and Behavior Books, 1981.

The Booze Battle: An Approach That Works. Ruth Maxwell. Praeger, 1976. Rev. Ballantine, 1986.

Beyond the Booze Battle. Ruth Maxwell. Ballantine, 1988.

Beyond Codependency. Melanie Beattie. Harper & Row, 1989.

Codependent No More. Melanie Beattie. Hazelden, 1986.

Chocolate to Morphine: Understanding Mind-Active Drugs. Andrew Weill, M.D., and Winifred Rosen. Houghton Mifflin, 1983.

The Courage to Change: Personal Conversations About Alcoholism. Dennis Wholey. Houghton Mifflin, 1984.

Crisis Intervention: Theory and Methodology. D. Aguilera and J. Messick. C. V. Mosby Company, 1978.

Dear Doc: A Noted Authority Answers Your Questions on Drinking and Drugs. Joseph Pursch, M.D. CompCare, 1985.

Drug and Alcohol Abuse: A Clinical Guide to Diagnosis and Treatment. Marc Schuckit, M.D. Plenum Publishing, 1984.

Eating Right to Live Sober. Katherine Ketcham and L. Ann Mueller, M.D. Madrona Publishers, 1985.

From Opium to Heroin (film). Cinemed Films, 1986.

Getting Them Sober. Toby Rice Drews. Bridge Publishing, 1980.

Grapevine, January, 1963. Alcoholics Anonymous.

The Haight Ashbury Cocaine Film: Physiology, Compulsion and Recovery. Cinemed, 1986.

I'll Quit Tomorrow. Vernon E. Johnson. Harper & Row, 1973, 1980.

Intervention: How to Help Someone Who Doesn't Want Help. Vernon E. Johnson. Johnson Institute Books, 1986; NAL, 1988.

Is Alcoholism Hereditary? Donald Goodwin, M.D. Oxford University Press, 1976; rev. paperback, Bantam, 1988.

The Little Red Book: An Orthodox Interpretation of the Twelve Steps. Hazelden, 1970.

Living on the Edge: A Guide to Intervention for Families with Drug and Alcohol Problems. Katherine Ketcham and Ginny Lyford Gustafson. Bantam Books, 1989.

Low Blood Sugar and You. Carlton Fredericks, M.D., and Herman Goodman. Ace Books, 1983.

A Matter of Balance: The Psychology and Brain Chemistry of Psychoactive Drugs (film). Cinemed, 1987.

Mind, Mood and Medicine. Paul H. Wender, M.D., and Donald F. Klein, M.D. NAL, 1982.

"New Insights into the Causes of Alcoholism." Kenneth Blum and Michael Trachtenberg. *Professional Counselor*, March/April 1987.

Not-God: A History of Alcoholics Anonymous. Ernest Kurtz. Hazelden, 1979.

On Death and Dying (for understanding the emotions caused by sudden changes in personal relationships). Elisabeth Kübler-Ross. Macmillan Publishing, 1970.

One Day at a Time in Al-Anon. Al-Anon Family Group Headquarters, 1968.

Peoplemaking. Virginia Satir. Science and Behavior Books, 1972.

Please Understand Me: Character and Temperament Types. David Keirsey and Marilyn Bates. Prometheus Nemesis, 1978.

Recovery: How to Get and Stay Sober. L. Ann Mueller and Katherine Ketcham. Bantam, 1987.

Reality Therapy: A New Approach to Psychiatry. William Glasser, M.D. Harper & Row, 1975.

The Search for Serenity and How to Achieve It. Lewis F. Presnall. U.A.F. Publishing, 1959.

The Secret of Staying in Love (communication skills/handling emotions). John Powell. Tabor, 1974.

Smokable Cocaine: The Haight Ashbury Crack Film. Cinemed, 1989.

Stage II Recovery: Life Beyond Addiction. Ernie Larsen. Harper & Row, 1985.

Time Is All We Have. Barnaby Conrad. Morrow, 1986.

To Care Enough: Intervention with Chemically Dependent Colleagues. Linda R. Crosby, M.S.N., R.N., and LeClair Bissell, M.D., C.A.C.

Unconditional Love (understanding emotions/acceptance). John Powell. Tabor, 1978.

Under the Influence: A Guide to the Myths and Realities of Alcoholism. James R. Milam and Katherine Ketcham. Madrona Publishers, 1981; paperback edition, Bantam, 1987.

Uppers, Downers, All Arounders: Physical and Mental Effects of Psychoactive Drugs. Darryl S. Inaba, Pharm.D., and William E. Cohen. Cinemed, 1989.

Where Did Everybody Go? Paul Molloy. Warner Books, 1982.

Women Who Love Too Much. Robin Norwood. Pocket Books, 1986.

Index

◆

abstinence, 70
abuse, indicators of, 16
abuse stage, 28, 56
acceptance stage, 141, 142
accreditation of treatment programs, 83
ActionStyles, 120–27
  in dysfunctional family, 137, 138
  intervening in, 128–29
addiction, 15
  abstinence from, 70
  as allergic disease, 42–43
  classes of, 55
  dependency distinguished from, 29
  endorphins and, 46
  evidence of, 23
  extent of, 54
  as final stage of dependency, 28–29, 56
  impotency and frigidity in, 158
  medically based treatment programs for, 79
  misconceptions regarding, 33
  moral character and, 53
  personal responsibility and, 53
  signs of, 31
  stages of, 56
  willful misconduct and, 52
addiction psychosis, 51, 167
Adult Children of Alcoholics, 96

affirming step, in intervention, 112–14
age, tolerance differences and, 49–50
Al-Anon, 10–11, 83, 85, 96
Alateen, 96
alcohol
  age and abuse of, 50
  aphrodisiac effect of, 158
  brain membranes and, 50
  in cough medicines and mouthwashes, 162
  differences in tolerance for, 49
  as drug, 54–55
  social drinking and, 50
  warning signs of abuse of, 16–17
alcohol counselors, 86
Alcoholics Anonymous, 62, 63, 83–84, 136, 148, 168
alcoholism
  addiction psychosis and, 51
  as allergic disease, 42, 43
  averse drugs for, 82
  biology of, 44
  detoxification from, 35
  differences in tolerance for alcohol and, 49
  drug addiction and, 54–55
  dry drunks and, 70–71
  early treatment programs for, 78
  endorphins and, 46

alcoholism (*cont.*)
ethnic factors in, 47–48
heredity factors in, 45–46
hypoglycemia and, 48–49
life after recovery from, 157–64
medically based treatment programs for, 79
in multiple-abuse problems, 72
mutual aid support groups for, 83–85
social drinking leading to, 50
allergic disease, dependency as, 42–43
amphetamines
smokable, 35
warning signs of abuse of, 16–17
anger, 141, 161
answering services, 63, 84
Antabuse, 82
antihistamine abuse, 16–17
aphrodisiac effect of alcohol and drugs, 158
Asians (Orientals), 47
aversion therapy, 82–83

babies
as addicts, 72
as role for dependents, 138–39
barbiturate abuse, 16–17
behavior
in causes of dependency, 51
of dry drunks, 70–71
effects of dependency in, 32
evidence of dependency in, 23–24
willful misconduct, 52
behavioral treatment programs, 82–83
biological factors in dependency
age differences in, 49–50
allergic disease as, 42–43
brain membranes and, 50
endorphins and, 46
ethnicity and, 47–48
heredity in, 45–46
hypoglycemia and, 48–49
predispositions in, 45
psychology and, 43–44
tolerance differences in, 49
bodily evidence, 24
brain
alcohol and drug dependencies and, 54

alcohol's impact on, 44
endorphins and, 46
membranes of, 50
breathalizer tests, 23

cannabis, 16–17
CARE process in intervention, 109
affirming step in, 112–14
confronting step in, 109–11
dependent's personality style in, 119–20
enacting step in, 115–16
for explorer personality type, 126–27, 132–33
for harmonizer personality type, 120–22, 130–31
for organizer personality type, 122–23, 131–32
for performer personality type, 123–26, 132
responding step in, 114–15
causes of chemical dependency, 39–40
age differences in, 49–50
biological factors in, 42–44
brain membranes and, 50
emotional immaturity and, 53–54
endorphins and, 46
ethnicity and, 47–48
hereditary factors in, 45–46
hypoglycemia and, 48–49
moral character and, 53
personal responsibility and, 53
predispositions to, 45
psychological and behavioral factors in, 51
social, 40–41
social drinking and, 50
tolerance differences in, 49
willful misconduct and, 52
central nervous system, 25
see also brain
certified alcohol counselor (C.A.C.), 86
certified alcohol and drug counselor (C.A.D.C.), 86
certified drug counselor (C.D.C.), 86
certified employee assistance professional (C.E.A.P.), 86
chaplains, 87
chemical dependency, 14–15
abstinence from, 70
age differences in, 49–50

in babies, 72
biological factors in, 42–44
causes of, 39–41
co-dependency and, 95–96
confronting, 109–11
costs of, 22–23
effect on brain membranes of, 50
egotism in, 20–21
emotional immaturity and, 53–54
endorphins and, 46
ethnic factors in, 47–48
evidence of, 23–25
hereditary factors in, 45–46
hypoglycemia and, 48–49
identification of, 25–26
intervention in, 8
life after recovery from, 157–64
misconceptions about, 33–34
moral character and, 53
mutiple-abuse problems, 72
personal responsibility in, 53
predispositions to, 45
progression of, 34
psychological and behavioral
    factors in, 51
social drinking and, 50
stages of, 27–29
tolerance differences in, 49
understanding the dependent, 101–
    2
urge to control in, 19–20
warning signs of, 16–17
willful misconduct and, 52
chief enablers, 138–39
children
    as addicts, 72
    of alcoholics, 45–46
clergy, 87
closed meetings, 85
cocaine abuse
    addiction psychosis and, 51
    egotism in, 21
    smokable, 35
    warning signs of, 16–17
codeine abuse, 16–17
co-dependency, 14, 95–96
    in dysfunctional family, 138
communications in intervention, 107–
    18
    how much to tell, 154
community groups, 104
community intervention, 64–67, 100

community resources, 85–86
compulsive overeating, 48
concerned-other intervention, 6, 64–
    67
    planning sessions for, 98–100
    preparation for, 91–92
conditioning, 82
confidentiality
    in employment-related programs,
        164
    of medical reports, 24–25
    in twelve-step self-help programs,
        155
confronting, 109–11
    emotions in, 135–36
    responding to arguments in, 143–
        49
consultants, 58
    for employment-related programs,
        164
control, urge to, 19–20
corn, allergy to, 43
costs of chemical dependency, 22–23
cough medicines, alcohol in, 162
counseling model treatment pro-
    grams, 78–80
counselors, 58, 86
crisis centers, 104
custody, in ultimatums, 152
cutting down, 34

dehydrogenase, 49
denial of dependency, 141, 142
    in relapses, 162
dependency, 28
    addiction distinguished from, 29
    co-dependency and, 95–96
    progression of, 34
    signs of, 29, 32
    stages of, 30–31
    understanding the dependent, 101–
        2
    warning signs of, 16–17
    see also chemical dependency
depressants, abuse of, 16–17
depression, 118, 141
designer drugs, 72
detoxification, 35, 85
    in medically based treatment
        programs, 78, 79
    supervision for, 103
divorce, in ultimatums, 152

driving under the influence of alcohol
  breathalizer tests for, 23
  police reports of, 25
drug counselors, 86
drugs
  aphrodisiac effect of, 158
  averse, 82
  designer drugs, 72
  effects and side effects of, 25–26
  endogenous and exogenous, 40–41
  fast-acting, 34–35
  hiding places for, 24
  prescription painkillers, 161–62
  warning signs of abuse of, 16–17
drug tests, 23
dry drunks, 70–71
dysfunctional family, 136–40

eating disorders, 48
egotism, 20–21
emergency medical technologists, 104
emotions
  of confronter, 135–36
  of dependents, 140–42
  of dry drunks, 70–71
  immaturity in, 53–54
  after recovery, 160–61
employment
  costs of chemical dependency in,
    22–23
  counseling in, 85
  documentation of abuse problems
    in, 25
  drug tests in, 23
  in effective ultimatums, 152
  recovery encouraged by, 163–64
enablers, 94
enacting step, in intervention, 115–16
endogenous drugs, 40
endorphins, 46
ethnicity, 47–48
evidence of chemical dependency, 23–
  25
exogenous drugs, 40–41
experimentation stage, 28, 56
explorers (personality style), 126–27
  CARE steps for intervention in,
    128–29
  healthy and dependent charts for,
    124–25
  intervening with, 132–33
  profile of, 121

Families Anonymous, 96
family
  co-dependency and, 95–96
  dysfunctional, 136–40
  signs of dependency in, 30–31
family counseling, 96
family heroes, 139
fast-acting drugs, 34–35
fears
  of dependents, 141
  in intervention, 93–95
fees for professional counseling, 60
financial signs of dependency, 30–31
French people, 47
friends, after recovery, 160
frigidity, 158
full-performance recovery, 73–74

"geographics," 19
Goodwin, Donald, 45–46
grieving process, 141–42

hallucinogens, 16–17
harmonizers (personality style), 120–
  22
  CARE steps for intervention in,
    128–29
  healthy and dependent charts for,
    124–25
  intervening with, 130–31
hashish
  addiction psychosis and, 51
  warning signs of abuse, 16–17
healing process, 141–42
hereditary factors in dependency, 45–
  46
heroin
  methadone and, 55
  warning signs of addiction to, 16–
    17
hiding places for drugs, 24
hospitals, 104
hot lines, 63
humor, 11
hypoglycemia, 48–49

identification of chemical dependency, 25–26
immaturity, 53–54
  after recovery, 161
impotency, 158
Indians (Native Americans), 47
inhalant abuse, 16–17

inheritance, in ultimatums, 152
insurance, 60, 164
intervention, 57–58
  co-dependency and, 95–96
  communications in, 107–18
  by concerned others, 64–67
  definition of, 5
  errors in, 26
  evidence in, 23
  for fast-acting drugs, 34–35
  humor in, 11
  in medically based treatment
    programs, 79
  mutual aid groups for, 61–64
  objectives of, 103
  personality style of dependents in,
    119–33
  planning sessions for, 97–100
  preparation for, 91–95
  professional, 58–61
  resentment of, 10
  teams for, 96–97
  timing of, 101
  types of, 6
  ultimatums in, 152–53
  understanding the dependent in,
    101–2
  where and how, 102–3
  as win-win situation, 8
investments, in ultimatums, 153
Irish people, 47
Italians, 47

Jews, 47
Johnson, Vernon, 64
Joint Commission on Accreditation of
  Health Care Institutions, 83
judges, 105
Jung, Carl, 39, 71
junk food, 32

Ketcham, Katherine, 44
Kübler-Ross, Elisabeth, 140

law enforcement, costs of chemical
  dependency to, 22
legal issues
  for employers, 25
  signs of dependency, 30–31
  slander suits, 26
lies, 154
listening, 112–13

Lombardi, Vince, 143
lost child role, 139
lovers, ultimatums from, 152–53
low blood sugar (hypoglycemia), 48–
  49
LSD, 16–17

maintenance programs, 70
manipulation, 141
marijuana
  age differences and, 50
  warning signs of abuse of, 16–17
mascot role, 140
medically based treatment programs,
  78–80
medical reports, 24–25
mental effects of dependency, 32
mental health centers, 86–87
mental illness, addiction as, 81
mental signs of dependency, 30–31
mescaline, 16–17
methadone, 55
methamphetamine abuse, 35
methaqualone abuse, 16–17
misconceptions regarding chemical
  abuse, 33–34
moral character, 53
morphine abuse, 16–17
motives for intervention, 92–93
mouthwashes, alcohol in, 162
Mueller, Ann, 44
multiple-abuse problems, 72
mushrooms, hallucinogenic, warning
  signs of, 16–17
mutual aid (self-help) groups, 61–64,
  136
  confidentiality in, 155

Nar-Anon, 96
narcotics, warning signs of addiction
  to, 16–17
Narcotics Anonymous (NA), 63, 83,
  148
Native Americans (Indians), 47
negotiations in intervention, 117
neurotransmitters, 40
  alcohol and, 44

occupational signs of dependency,
  30–31
open meetings, 84–85
opium, 16–17

organizers (personality style), 122–23
CARE steps for intervention in,
128–29
healthy and dependent charts for,
124–25
intervening with, 131
profile of, 121
Orientals (Asians), 47
overdoses, signs of, 17
ownership, in ultimatums, 153
Oxford Group, 71

painkilling drugs, 161–62
paranoia, 155, 167
paraphernalia, 24
Paul (saint), 167
PCP, 16–17, 35
penalties, in ultimatums, 116
perfectionism, 93
performers (personality style), 123–26
CARE steps for intervention in,
128–29
intervening on, 131–32
profile of, 121
personality styles of dependents, 119–
20
explorers, 126–27
harmonizers, 120–22
organizers, 122–23
performers, 123–26
personal responsibility, 53, 101
phenmetrazine abuse, 16–17
physical effects of dependency, 32
physical signs of dependency, 30–31
physicians, 105
"pink clouding," 163
planning sessions, for interventions,
97–100
police, 104
in ultimatums, 153
police reports, 25
political issues, 48
powerlessness state, 28–29, 40
predispositions to dependency, 45
hypoglycemia and, 48–49
preoccupation stage, 28
prescription painkillers, 161–62
prison, in ultimatums, 153
private therapists, 86–87
professional intervention, 58–61
alcohol and drug counselors, 86

following suicide warning signs,
66–67
private therapists and mental
health centers, 86–87
programs for living, 70–71
propellant abuse, 16–17
psychiatric treatment programs, 80–
82
psychiatrists, 105
psychoanalysis, 81
psychological factors in dependency,
51
biology and, 43–44
psychologists, 58, 86, 105
psychoses, 26, 51, 81, 167
punishment, 58

Queen Isabella Syndrome, 96

recovery, 40, 69–75
abilities after, 157–58
from alcohol and drug dependencies, 54
detachment and, 171–72
employment and, 163–64
healing and grieving process in,
141–42
objectives of, 103
rewards of, 165–68
sex life after, 158–59
social life after, 159, 160
treatment programs for, 78–83
Recovery Ultimatums, 115–16
effective, 152–54
recreational use, 28
rehabilitation programs, drug testing
in, 23
relapses, 153
avoiding, 163
signs of, 162
religious outreach groups, 104
reputations, in ultimatums, 153
resistance to help, 93–95
responding step, in intervention, 114–
15
responses to dependents' arguments,
143–49
rewards, in ultimatums, 116
roles, in intervention, 94

Satir, Virginia, 138
scapegoat role, 139

secondary addictions, 81
sedative abuse, 35
selection of treatment programs, 83
self-control, 52, 58
self-help (mutual aid) groups, 61–64,
    83–85, 136
  confidentiality in, 155
Serenity Prayer, 20
sex life after recovery, 158–59
Shakespeare, William, 165
shock therapy, 82
slander suits, 26
sleeping-pill abuse, 35
SOBER listening, 112
social drinking, 50
social factors
  in causes of dependency, 40–41
  ethnicity and, 47–48
  in signs of dependency, 30–31
social life after recovery, 159, 160
social service agencies, 104
social service reports, 25
social workers, 58, 86
"soft" intervention, 61–63
solvent abuse, 16–17
spiritual factors in recovery, 71–72
  chaplains for, 87
  in medically based treatment
      programs, 78, 79
spouses, co-dependency among, 96
stages of dependency, 27–31, 56
stimulant abuse, 16–17
sugar, hypoglycemia and, 48–49
suicide, 118
  warning signs of, 66–67

teams, in intervention, 96–97
  procedures for, 108–16
tetrahydroisoquinolines (TIQ's), 46,
    55
THC, 16–17
therapy, 59
tolerance
  age differences and, 49–50
  in alcoholics, 44
  differences in, 49
tranquilizer abuse

detoxification from, 35
  warning signs of, 16–17
treatment programs, 59–60, 78
  for alcoholism, 48
  behavioral and aversion therapy,
      82–83
  community resources for, 85–86
  confidentiality in, 155
  intimacy in, 163
  medically based counseling model
      for, 78–80
  mutual aid support groups as, 83–
      85
  by private therapists and mental
      health centers, 86–87
  psychiatric model for, 80–82
  selection of, 83
treatment and recovery centers, 104
Tutu, Desmond, 154
twelve-step self-help programs, 62,
    83–85
  confidentiality in, 155
  for family members, 96
  in medically based treatment
      programs, 79

ultimatums, 99, 115–16
  effective, 152–54
use stage, 28, 56

Valium, 55
violence, 104, 118

waiting lists for treatments, 60
walk-in clinics, 104
warning signs
  of chemical abuse, 16–17
  of suicide, 66–67
Wegscheider, Sharon, 138
withdrawal, 33
  signs of, 17
  supervision for, 103
women
  alcohol dependency among, 49
  eating disorders among, 48

About the Authors

Bob Wright and Deborah George Wright are uniquely qualified to write a consumer's intervention manual: they are educational and communications specialists in substance-abuse prevention, intervention and treatment. Together, they have over thirty years of technical and teaching experience in the field of human development. Bob is a recovering alcoholic with ten years' sobriety and Deborah is a recovering family member—a co-dependent—with eight years in recovery. They have developed and applied their techniques for constructive confrontation in hundreds of interventions. The Wrights are the founders of Recovery Communications, a national consulting company specializing in material for intervention programs for home, workplace and education. They offer seminars to businesses, civic organizations, school systems, colleges and church groups, advise treatment centers, and provide training necessary for the continued certification of alcohol and drug counselors.

Additional copies of *Dare to Confront!* may be ordered by sending a check for $17.95 (please add the following for postage and handling: $1.50 for the first copy, $.50 for each added copy) to:

MasterMedia Limited
16 East 72nd Street
New York, NY 10021
(212) 260-5600
(800) 334-8232

Bob Wright and Deborah George Wright are available for speeches and workshops. Please contact MasterMedia's Speakers' Bureau for availability and fee arrangements. Call Tony Colao at (201) 359-1612.

Other MasterMedia Books

THE PREGNANCY AND MOTHERHOOD DIARY: Planning the First Year of Your Second Career, by Susan Schiffer Stautberg, is the first and only undated appointment diary that shows how to manage pregnancy and career. ($12.95 spiralbound)

◆

CITIES OF OPPORTUNITY: Finding the Best Place to Work, Live and Prosper in the 1990's and Beyond, by Dr. John Tepper Marlin, explores the job and living options for the next decade and into the next century. This consumer guide and handbook, written by one of the world's experts on cities, selects and features forty-six American cities and metropolitan areas. ($13.95 paper, $24.95 cloth)

◆

THE DOLLARS AND SENSE OF DIVORCE: The Financial Guide for Women, by Judith Briles, is the first book to combine practical tips on overcoming the legal hurdles with planning finances before, during and after divorce. ($10.95 paper)

◆

OUT THE ORGANIZATION: How Fast Could You Find a New Job?, by Madeleine and Robert Swain, is written for the millions of Americans whose jobs are no longer safe, whose companies are not loyal and who face futures of uncertainty. It gives advice on finding a new job or starting your own business. ($11.95 paper, $17.95 cloth)

◆

AGING PARENTS AND YOU: A Complete Handbook to Help You Help Your Elders Maintain a Healthy, Productive and Independent Life, by Eugenia Anderson-Ellis and Marsha Dryan, is a complete guide to providing care to aging relatives. It gives practical advice and resources to the adults who are helping their elders lead productive and independent lives. ($9.95 paper)

◆

CRITICISM IN YOUR LIFE: How to Give It, How to Take It, How to Make It Work for You, by Dr. Deborah Bright, offers practical advice, in an upbeat, readable and realistic fashion, for turning criticism into control. Charts and diagrams guide the reader into managing criticism from bosses, spouses, children, friends, neighbors, and in-laws. ($9.95 paper, $17.95 cloth)

◆

BEYOND SUCCESS: How Volunteer Service Can Help You Begin Making a Life Instead of Just a Living, by John F. Raynolds III and Eleanor Raynolds, C.B.E., is a unique how-to book targeted to business and professional people considering volunteer work, senior citizens who wish to fill leisure time meaningfully and students trying out various career options. The book is filled with interviews with celebrities, CEOs and average citizens who talk about the benefits of service work. ($9.95 paper, $19.95 cloth)

◆

MANAGING IT ALL: Time-Saving Ideas for Career, Family, Relationships and Self, by Beverly Benz Treuille and Susan Schiffer Stautberg, is written for women who are juggling careers and families. Over two hundred career women (ranging from a TV anchorwoman to an investment banker) were interviewed. The book contains many humorous anecdotes on saving time and improving the quality of life for self and family. ($9.95 paper)

◆

REAL LIFE 101: (Almost) Surviving Your First Year Out of College, by Susan Kleinman, supplies welcome advice to those facing "real life" for the first time, focusing on work, money, health and how to deal with freedom and responsibility. ($9.95 paper)

◆

YOUR HEALTHY BODY, YOUR HEALTHY LIFE: How to Take Control of Your Medical Destiny, by Donald B. Louria, M.D., provides precise advice and strategies that will help you to live a long and healthy life. Learn also about nutrition, exercise, vitamins and medication, as well as how to control risk factors for major diseases. ($12.95 paper)

◆

THE CONFIDENCE FACTOR: How Self-Esteem Can Change Your Life, by Judith Briles, is based on a nationwide survey of six thousand men and women. Briles explores why women so often feel a lack of self-confidence and have a poor opinion of themselves. She offers step-by-step advice on becoming the person you want to be. ($18.95 cloth)

◆

THE SOLUTION TO POLLUTION: 101 Things You Can Do to Clean Up Your Environment, by Laurence Sombke, offers step-by-step techniques on how to conserve more energy, start a recycling center, choose biodegradable products and how to proceed with individual environmental cleanup projects. ($7.95 paper)

◆

TAKING CONTROL OF YOUR LIFE: The Secrets of Successful Enterprising Women, by Gail Blanke and Kathleen Walas, is based on the authors' professional experience with Avon Products' Women of Enterprise Awards, given each year to outstanding women entrepreneurs. The authors offer a specific plan to help you gain control over your life and include business tips and quizzes as well as beauty and lifestyle information. ($17.95 cloth)

◆

POWER PARTNERS: How Two-Career Couples Can Play to Win, by Jane Hershey Cuozzo and S. Diane Graham, describes how two-career couples can learn the difference between competing with a spouse and becoming a supportive Power Partner. ($19.95 cloth)